# the taylor lautner album

## amy carpenter

plexus, london

# the taylor lautner album

# contents

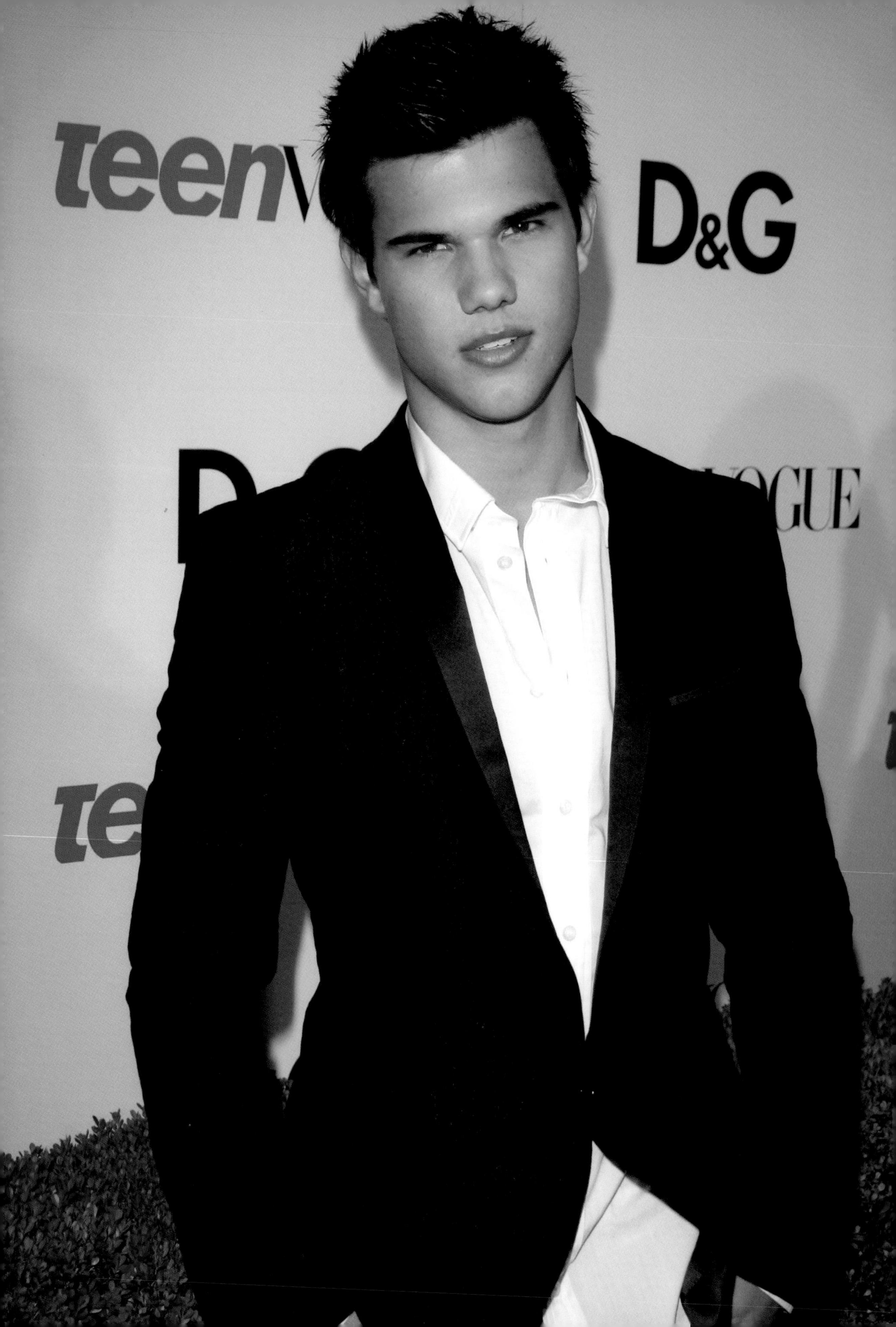
teen
D&G

# introduction

'Personally, I don't get the vampire thing.
They're cold, werewolves are hot. I mean,
cold, hot . . . come on! . . . The Team
Edward fans, they'll come around.'
– Taylor Lautner

In the words of *New Moon*'s concussed, confused heroine Bella Swan, there's no denying that Taylor Lautner is 'sort of beautiful'. With intense brown eyes, the most infectious smile in Hollywood and a body to die for, Taylor is the smouldering young star who has left a generation of teens – to say nothing of their mothers – dreaming of romantic nights lost beneath silver moons. Two thousand and eight was the year he shot to fame as troubled teen werewolf Jacob Black in the first cinematic instalment of Stephenie Meyer's *Twilight Saga*. Since then, he's made the role his own. If there's one wolf who could steal Bella – along with the hearts of devoted *Twi*-fans everywhere – from the arms of Robert Pattinson's ice-cool vamp Edward Cullen, then it's Taylor, and with the release of *New Moon* he is poised to do exactly this. Yet in truth, Taylor is one young heartthrob who's fought for success fang and claw, every step of the way – demonstrating steely determination that belies his youth.

From the very earliest age, it was evident that Taylor Lautner was going to be *somebody*. He was a strikingly intelligent and well-behaved child, blessed with natural good looks and athleticism. The only real uncertainty about Taylor's future success was which of his many talents he would choose to develop.

Initially, he seemed set for a career as a sportsman. His innate talent for martial arts and extraordinary acrobatic skills combined with Taylor's nascent showmanship to make him a multiple world champion in a variety of martial arts disciplines before he was ten years old.

For most people, becoming a world champion in any field would represent the peak of a lifetime's achievement. But Taylor is a unique individual, whose precocious talents and formidable sense of self-discipline compelled him to explore every atom of his apparently limitless potential.

By the time he was in his teens, he had set aside performing and competing in martial arts to pursue a career as an actor. This entailed countless hours of travel, endless auditions,

*On a mission to mesmerise: fresh from filming in Vancouver, Taylor wows the crowds at*
*Teen Vogue's Seventh Annual Young Hollywood Party, September 2009.*

*Torn in two: 'Bella's still in love with Edward,' explained Taylor, 'but she's kind of fallen for Jacob, too.'*

'I met with the casting director, we talked, and she asked for some poses. It was funny though, because at the time, I didn't even know what a pose was . . . but I learned quickly.'
– Taylor Lautner

moving from his hometown to Los Angeles, and almost superhuman levels of application and commitment as he sought to balance the necessity to complete his education with attempting to break in to one of the most competitive professions in the world.

Thanks to the support of his family, his own drive and ambition, and an increasingly evident talent for acting, Taylor succeeded. Irrespective of his newfound fame and status he remains a polite, likeable teenager who refuses to let mass adulation go to his head. He remains unaffected, easygoing and approachable – and it is these qualities, as much as his many talents, that serve to mark him out as an exceptional role model.

Not yet out of his teens, Taylor is an established Hollywood star with a long and exciting future ahead of him. Yet he remains eager to hone his craft, develop his talents and assimilate new skills. He has expressed an interest in screenwriting and returning to sports, but for now he is an actor on the cusp of superstardom. Given his track record of unique achievement, who is to say where his talents will lead him in the future? One thing is for sure – the world will hear much more of Taylor Lautner, and for many years to come. 'As long as you like me best […] I'm prepared to be annoyingly persistent,' promises Jacob Black. Coming from Taylor Lautner, you know it's more than just a line.

*Taylor unleashes his own killer sense of style for the 2009 CFDA Fashion Awards in New York.*

# the k a r a t e kid

# I

'My main hero is my family;
they have been here since day one.'
– Taylor Lautner

For anyone who's imagined walking the frosted streets of Forks along with Edward, Bella and Jacob, Tuesday, 11 February 1992 was a day when you could truly believe you were there – and one Deborah and Daniel Lautner, a young couple from Grand Rapids, Michigan, would never forget. Miles from Jacob Black's hometown, the bitterly cold winter's morning heralded the birth of their first child – a baby boy with jet-black hair and warm russet eyes. They named him Taylor Daniel. As they broke the happy news to family and friends, this much was clear: the new arrival could be assured of all the love and attention that his excited, first-time parents had to give.

Growing up, Taylor's first home was on Rosewood Avenue, just a few blocks away from where future president Gerald Ford spent part of his childhood. It was a modest house, with little to mark it out from others along that leafy street, but for the newly-expanded Lautner family it was a happy home. Situated within the city's south-eastern suburbs, with an array of green spaces and schools to choose from, it was an ideal neighbourhood for any new parents looking to settle down and raise their children in safety.

Although Dan's work as a commercial airline pilot often called for long periods away from home, Deborah was employed by Herman Miller – an office design firm noted for a flexible and progressive approach to staff that enabled her to spend a good deal of time with baby Taylor. Both Deborah and Dan's families had lived in the region for many years, and although Dan's relations hailed from Traverse City, some one hundred and fifty miles north of Grand Rapids, Deborah's folks were a little closer to home in Manistee, Michigan.

Despite the extended Lautner family's willingness to help out with looking after the new arrival, the distance between Grand Rapids and Traverse City or Manistee meant daily commutes back and forth were simply not practical, and so baby Taylor was enrolled in one of the many local day-care facilities, where, long before *The Twilight Saga*, Taylor's inner wolf bared his teeth for the first time. 'I was a biter at day-care,' Taylor admitted in

*It could be you: young Taylor greets fans who turned out to
see him on the night of the* Sahara *premiere, April 2005.*

October 2008, flashing Terri Finch Hamilton – a reporter for the *Grand Rapids Press* – a particularly wolfish grin. 'I don't remember it, but my parents tell me I'd bite other kids.'

Although the family soon settled into a happy domestic routine, this was not to last. In 1996, when Taylor was just four years old, their house on Rosewood Avenue was gutted by fire. As luck would have it, Deborah had taken Taylor to stay at his aunt's for the night and Dan was away working, so despite the trauma of suddenly losing their home and many of their possessions, the Lautners had something of a lucky escape. 'The police called and told us our house had burned down,' Taylor recalled. 'If my aunt hadn't invited us to sleep over . . . well, wow.'

Dan, Deborah and Taylor moved into a new, more spacious house in Hudsonville, a neighbourhood some twenty miles south-west of their first home, which had the advantage of being closer to several of Taylor's aunts and uncles. Founded upon orchard farming, the city of Hudsonville was home to around six thousand people, many of whom had been attracted by the city's excellent selection of schools, parks and churches. The area was also known for producing a string of successful sports teams and professional sportsmen – a heritage that would help develop Taylor's growing interest in basketball, football and wrestling.

'I was a biter at day-care. I don't remember it, but my parents tell me I'd bite other kids.' – Taylor Lautner

Shortly after the move to Hudsonville, Deborah fell pregnant for a second time and in 1996 gave birth to a daughter, Makena. In *New Moon*, Jacob Black is described as Bella's 'own personal sun'. Representing warmth, light and hope, he's the only friend who can make her forget her nightmares and the gaping emptiness of life without Edward. And, in fact, six-and-a-half-year-old Taylor greeted his baby sister exactly as you'd expect, welcoming her to the family like a real-life version of his on-screen alter-ego. Having immediately hit it off, the siblings were to spend many hours playing happily together. 'My sister and I would always be spies when I was younger,' Taylor told *RadioFree.com*'s Michael J. Lee back in 2005. 'We'd be in the house, and I'd hide something, and I'd act like we were secret agents and spies. And I'd tell her that it was really happening, and she still believes me to this day. She's six. Pretty soon I gotta tell her that it's just fake and I'm trying to make her have fun.'

By now, Taylor had started school at nearby Jamestown Elementary, where his natural athleticism and aptitude for sports ensured that physical education was fast becoming his favourite subject. 'I did a lot of stuff in school,' he recalled in an interview with *eFilmCritic.com*'s Jason Whyte. 'I did wrestling, football, baseball, martial arts and before long, I was forced to narrow things down because you just can't do everything.'

Inspired by stories of family friends who had taken up karate, Taylor trained his focus on martial arts and began attending Fabiano's Karate and Fitness Centre in the nearby town of Holland. Run by Sensei Tom Fabiano, the centre is well established, with an excellent record of introducing youngsters to a wide range of martial arts disciplines.

*Taylor works the red carpet at the* Sahara *premiere, 2005, showcasing the same jaw-dropping move that first caught the eye of* Sharkboy *director Robert Rodriguez.*

Taylor joined Fabiano's 'Little Dragons' class, a programme designed specifically to be child-friendly, allowing four- to six-year-olds to learn martial arts in a nurturing environment. Fabiano places great emphasis on teaching the Matsumura Seito Shorin Ryu method, a form of karate that combines a traditional Okinawan fighting style with an emphasis on skill, precision and agility over strength. The school teaches two basic creeds: firstly, 'I intend to develop myself in a positive manner, and avoid anything that would reduce my mental growth or my physical health,' and secondly, 'I intend to develop self-discipline in order to bring out the best in myself and others.' Instilling a strong sense of commitment in all his pupils, Fabiano's doctrine laid the foundations for each and every one of Taylor's future successes.

'My mom's bosses' kids were doing martial arts, and since they were doing it, I just wanted to try it. So I started […] and it was a lot of fun,' Taylor explained to the *Kidzworld. com* website. 'Except for the part about being barefoot. I don't like being barefoot. I don't even wear sandals.' But, whatever his footwear requirements, it seems wild-boy Taylor was always destined to run with the pack. 'I really liked class because of all the games we got to play, like "swords and spears", "sensei says",' Taylor told *karateangels.com*. 'I didn't really care too much for the push-ups and all the hard work. I really started because of the fun games.'

Despite his mild aversion to the more strenuous aspects of the discipline, Taylor's best qualities – the natural drive, confidence and dedication that were soon to become his trademark – were already beginning to shine through. 'A lot of boys that age are bouncing off the walls, but Taylor was always deliberate, focused,' recalled Tom Fabiano. 'He wasn't a typical kid. He always worked extra hard.'

Soon enough, Taylor had grasped the fundamentals of Fabiano's philosophy, proving himself more than ready to graduate to the Children's Class, on a learning curve so steep

*A prickly-headed Taylor celebrates the release of* Ladder 49 *on DVD, March 2005, proving his taste for romance and real-life heroics is nothing new.*

it was headed through the ceiling. One year later, Sensei Fabiano had seen enough. Convinced his young charge was ready to compete on a national level, he entered Taylor for a championship set to take place in Louisville, Kentucky.

As competitive sporting debuts go, Taylor's was something truly spectacular – he triumphed in three separate disciplines, more than surpassing Tom Fabiano's wildest expectations and catching the eye of Mike Chat, a professional martial arts competitor and instructor with over fifty international championship wins on his résumé.

Born Michael Chaturantabut in Rayong Province, Thailand, twenty-four-year-old Chat had already made a formidable name for himself. A three-time World Forms and Weapons Champion and five-time North American Forms and Weapons Champion, he had also been inducted into the World Martial Arts Hall of Fame in 1992, aged just seventeen. Chat had developed a unique, charismatic fighting style, which combined traditional Okinawan Shorei-Ryu, Tae Kwon Do, Chinese Wushu, kickboxing, yoga, dance, ballet, and acrobatics to create a system which he dubbed 'extreme martial arts' (XMA). In addition to forming Team Chat Elite and International – two squads of martial artists trained in XMA who competed and gave exhibitions across the globe – Chat ran martial arts summer camps and had recently begun bringing his skills to wider audiences via Fox Network's popular TV show *WMAC Masters*. Thanks to the success of this series, Chat was in demand for appearances in TV ads, music videos, stunt doubling for Paolo Montalban in the *Mortal Kombat: Conquest* television series, and several small roles alongside the likes of Hong Kong movie legend Sammo Hung in his popular CBS show *Martial Law*.

In martial arts circles, Mike Chat was already a superstar and – although he achieved wider fame as Chad Lee, the blue Lightspeed Power Ranger in 2000's incarnation of the Power Rangers TV franchise, *Power Rangers: Lightspeed Rescue* – when Taylor first encountered him in 1999, he was still one of the boy's most inspiring personal heroes. Yet, if Taylor was left somewhat awestruck by the experience, he wasn't the only one.

Impressed by Taylor's precocious talents, Chat invited him to attend his Camp Chat International summer school at UCLA. The varied training programme drew upon elements of martial arts, gymnastics, acrobatics, stunt training, and the performing arts – all disciplines that suited Taylor's natural abilities, equipping him with invaluable skills that would stand him in good stead for the future. 'I fell in love,' Taylor recalled. 'By the end of the camp, I was doing aerial cartwheels with no hands.'

Taylor's tenure at Camp Chat only served to validate Mike's initial opinion of the young martial artist from Michigan. From that point on, Mike took over from Tom Fabiano as Taylor's instructor and set about the exhausting process of honing his pupil's raw talent to world-class standard.

The main difficulty facing both master and student was that of geography – Mike's touring and television commitments meant travelling to Hudsonville would never have been a viable option for him. Taylor's studies were also a priority, and so a compromise was struck, whereby Taylor travelled to Los Angeles to hook up with Mike whenever the opportunity arose. 'I try to get with my instructor, Mike Chat, as much as possible. He gives me homework assignments to work on at home. Then I go out with my mom and dad's help in trying to achieve my homework from Mike,' Taylor revealed.

'I didn't really care too much for the push-ups and all the hard work.
I really started because of the fun games.'
– Taylor Lautner

The demands of keeping on top of a programme of rigorous physical training while simultaneously managing to make progress in the classroom would be enough to challenge any pupil. Yet at the tender age of eight, Taylor was already juggling these apparently conflicting obligations with aplomb. Certainly, the standard of his schoolwork was showing no sign of slipping. 'I get mostly As with an occasional A minus here and there,' explained Taylor. 'The key is an open communication with my teacher. My parents and me are in close communication with my teachers to make sure I'm not missing anything and understanding assignments. This doesn't mean it's not been difficult, because it has. I think once the school understands that my education is important to me, and then they are more understanding. The last week has been really tough. I've had to stay up 'til 10:30 or 11:00pm each night to make sure all my homework is done.'

Aside from his martial arts prowess, it was Taylor's drive and mature attitude to an increasingly hectic lifestyle that served to mark him out as a unique individual. He was also highly inventive, and quickly began creating his own XMA moves. 'It's called a corkscrew,' he declared. 'It's a backflip off one leg and then you do a three-sixty in the air and I land it in the splits. I was the first competitor to ever land that in the national karate circuit.'

Such innate athleticism ensured that Taylor was a natural for XMA, thriving on the wide palette of influences inherent in his chosen discipline. 'Regular martial arts is traditional, with no music and no flips choreographed into it,' explained Taylor. 'But extreme martial arts is choreographed to music. It's very fast-beat up-tempo and you put a lot of acrobatic manoeuvres into the routine.'

Additionally, Taylor pursued his interest in football, squeezing games in around his already crowded timetable. 'My training schedule changes depending on the time of year. I try to train three to four times a week, but during football season, four times per week could be a little tough to fit in.'

Perhaps unsurprisingly, Taylor's speed and agility ensured that he was a good footballer and he followed the professional game with keen interest. 'My favourite college team is the Michigan Wolverines because I was born and raised in Michigan. And they're actually pretty good too! As for NFL, I don't really have a favourite. I like the Atlanta Falcons because I think Michael Vick is really, really good. And I like the Philadelphia Eagles,' he told *Oregon Herald* journalist Mark Sells in 2005.

Taylor was also a keen basketball fan, catching NBA games whenever his demanding schedule allowed. 'We try to be Detroit fans, but it's really tough,' he observed. 'We are however, big Detroit Pistons fans, who were champions last year and are in the finals this year. And I can't wait to watch them play the [San Antonio] Spurs.'

After scoring his black belt and being selected for the national karate team, Taylor was proud to represent his country for the first time at the 2000 World Karate Federation Championships. Pint-sized Taylor was entered in the category of boys under twelve years, giving many of his rivals a significant age advantage over him. Despite this handicap, Taylor proved he had the edge and fought off fierce competition to win three gold medals – making him a world champion several times over before he even reached the age of nine.

> 'I fell in love. By the end of the camp, I was doing aerial cartwheels with no hands.'
> – Taylor Lautner

Characteristically, irrespective of the praise his precocious talents were generating, Taylor stuck to the same intensive training schedule as before. Never one to let his aspirations slide out of focus, he set his sights on finishing his education, simply refusing to let success go to his head. As for using his lethal skills to settle schoolyard scores, Taylor has shown that he's hardly the type. 'It's never really happened,' he shrugged. 'Nobody's ever wanted to start a fight. I stay away from all that stuff.'

In addition to being technically excellent, Taylor's own personal brand of combat – with more than a few literal twists, flips and splits thrown in for good measure – also made for breathtaking entertainment, and he soon began appearing at demonstrations and exhibitions as part of Team Chat International. It was becoming increasingly apparent: Taylor Lautner was on course for a glittering career as the next hero of martial arts. On an unstoppable rise, the future he'd worked for seemed close enough to touch. And then Mike Chat suggested that Taylor took up acting.

The link between motion pictures and martial arts is long established and can be traced back more than fifty years to legendary director Akira Kurosawa's 1954 classic *Seven Samurai*. The movie – remade for American audiences as 1960's western *The Magnificent Seven* – set in motion a sequence of events that would culminate in Bruce Lee's ascent to global stardom in the early 1970s. Since Lee's mysterious and sudden death in 1973, a string of martial artists and pseudo-martial artists have found fame and fortune showcasing their skills on the silver screen.

Over time, the link between martial arts and cinema has become deeply embedded in

*Before he discovered the gym: Sweet but scrawny Taylor strikes a pose at the* Sahara *premiere.*

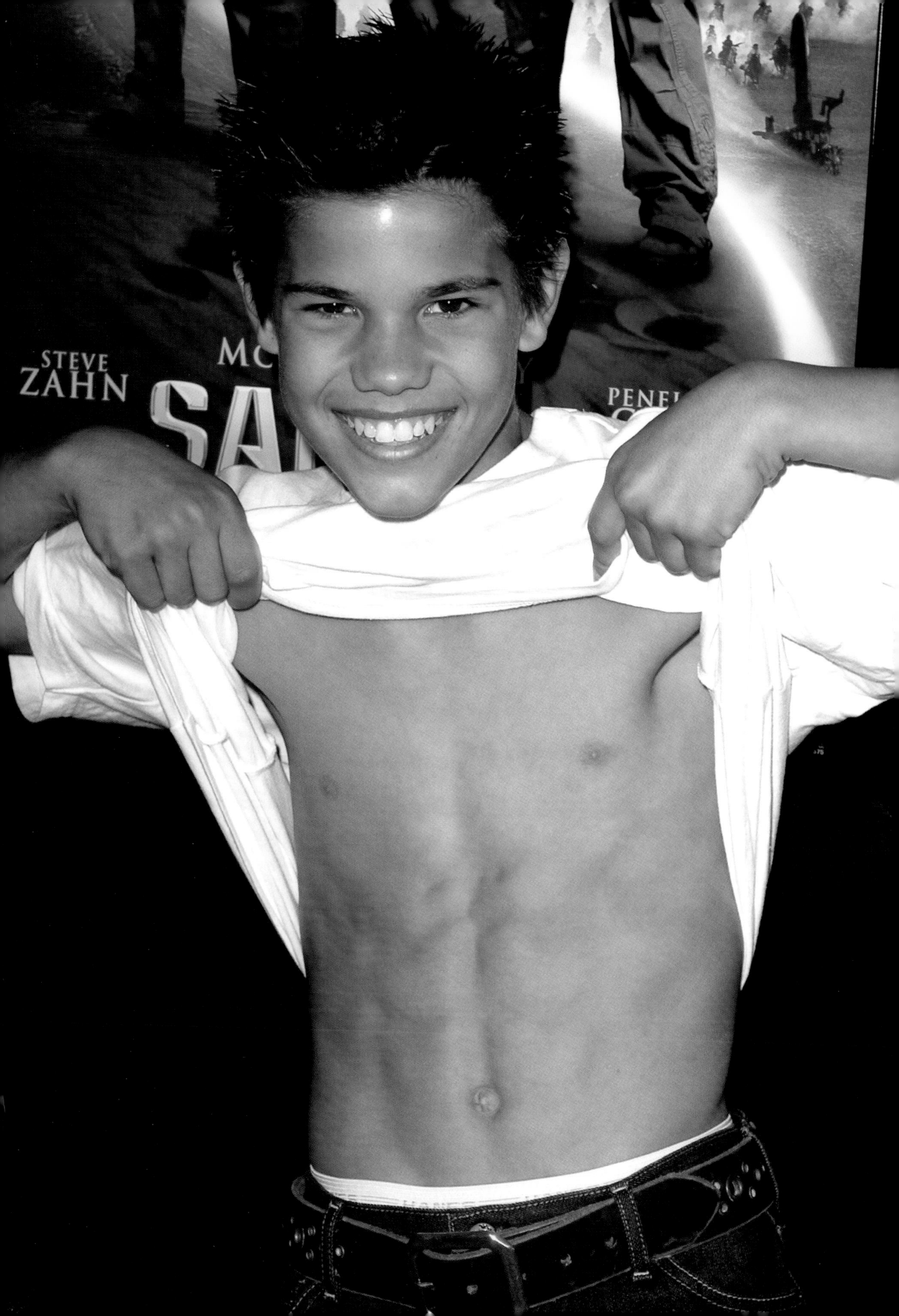
STEVE
ZAHN

popular culture and Taylor, like most boys with any interest in either, was keenly aware of this. Asked by *karateangels.com* whether he envisaged a career as the 'next Jean-Claude Van Damme', Taylor replied, 'I'd love to be an action director or writer or be in action films, just like him.'

'One of my favourite movies is *The Last Samurai* with Tom Cruise,' Taylor told *Ultimatedisney.com*'s Renata Joy. 'I love that movie. I guess I kind of like it because I can relate to it. I started out with the traditional Japanese martial arts and then I went into the extreme new modern version. In that movie, they started out with the samurai and the traditional fighting in war, and then they go to the more modern one. So I guess I could relate to it well and it just got me really in the moment. And I thought that Tom Cruise did a great job portraying that role.'

Having successfully combined a career as a professional martial artist with a plethora of on-screen cameos, Mike Chat knew better than most what directors and producers were looking for. Soon he realised Taylor had it in spades. 'He saw that I wasn't shy, that I was confident, that I talked a lot,' explained the young champion.

Anxious for others to see it too, Mike convinced Deb and Dan that the best approach would be to begin sending his young pupil to auditions in Hollywood. These would raise his profile, gradually making Taylor's a familiar face on the circuit, and hopefully pay off in the form of some bookings. Once again, any additional trips to Los Angeles would need to be slotted in around Taylor's scholastic obligations and training regime.

> 'He saw that I wasn't shy, that I was confident, that I talked a lot.'
> – Taylor Lautner

'The first audition that my karate instructor sent me out on was a Burger King commercial. It was kind of like a karate audition in that they were basically looking for martial arts stuff. And they were looking for someone older, but he wanted to send me anyway to get the experience,' recalled Taylor. 'I met with the casting director, we talked, and she asked for some poses. It was funny though, because at the time, I didn't even know what a pose was . . . but I learned quickly and did some poses for them. And I really liked it. I thought it went well, but I didn't get it.'

To break into such a fiercely competitive field as acting, Taylor would need every bit of his drive and dedication. Crucially, his positive attitude played an important role as the weeks passed and he travelled back and forth to LA without landing a single job. He began travelling to California on a monthly basis and soon became a familiar face among the many hopefuls scrambling desperately for the few roles that were on offer.

Despite the exhausting hours of travel and the ruthless nature of the auditions cattle market, Taylor never gave in to disappointment. Far from becoming disheartened, he held on to his enthusiasm to the very last. The self-discipline and focus taught by his sensei served him well – his mind was made up: he was going to become an actor. Though Taylor's own determined resolve and inner strength were enough to get him through, he could also count on the support of his parents. Hugely impressed by the dedication and effort Taylor was putting into pursuing his goal, Dan and Deborah began considering a move to Los Angeles. For the sake of their son's future, it was a chance they were willing to take.

*Disarming, charming Taylor – seen here at the* Cheaper By The Dozen 2 *premiere in December 2005 – has little in common with the schoolyard bullies he played early on in his career.*

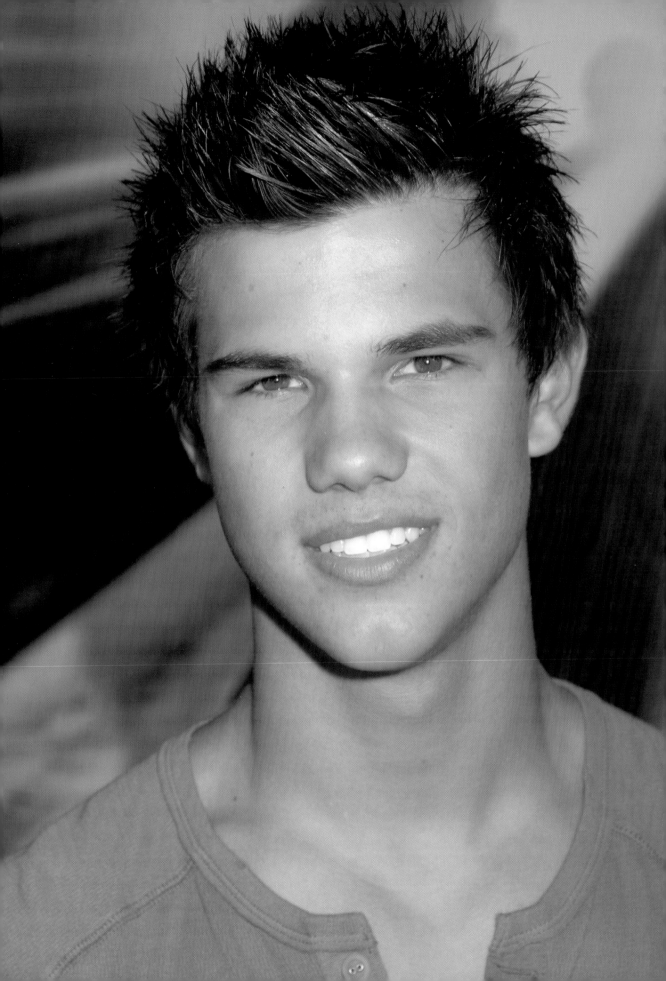

# just waiting 2

'I was forced to narrow things down because
you just can't do everything.'
– Taylor Lautner

Aside from the practical issues of relocating more than two thousand miles from Michigan to California, the Lautner family had to contend with the emotional wrench of leaving behind family, friends, and everything they'd known. It says much for Dan and Deborah's belief in their son's talent that they were prepared to back him to such an extent. But, in fact, the evidence in support of their decision was strong – one only had to consider the manner in which Taylor had mastered martial arts to realise that he was an exceptional talent. Also, the degree to which his parents were prepared to assist him in pursuing his latest ambition was more than matched by Taylor's determination to succeed.

Given that the family were committed to helping Taylor carve out a niche as an actor, moving to Los Angeles was the only practical option. As Taylor explained to *Grand Rapids Press* journalist Terri Finch Hamilton, 'They'd call at 9:00 or 10:00 at night, which was 6:00 or 7:00 their time, and say, "We've got an audition tomorrow – can you be here?" We'd leave really early in the morning and get there about noon. I'd go to the audition in the afternoon, take the red-eye back to Grand Rapids then go to school.'

Obviously, the expense, energy and time consumed by constant travelling back and forth across the country were part of a lifestyle the Lautners could never have maintained, as Deborah and Dan knew only too well. 'It was a very, very hard decision,' admitted Taylor in an interview with the *Oregon Herald*'s Mark Sells. 'Our family and friends did not want us to go. But our choices were: we could stay in Michigan and I could give up acting – I would have had to because it would have been crazy to continually fly out from Michigan to California each time there was an audition – or we could move to California and I could continue to act. I told my parents I didn't want to give up acting. And after weighing the good with bad, they agreed to move.'

Initially, the family opted for a trial period, waiting one month to see how things

*Payne for pleasure: Self-confessed action-addict Taylor attends
the premiere of violent thriller* Max Payne *in Los Angeles, October 2008.*

progressed. Then they would decide whether or not to make the move permanent. 'We came out for a month to train with my karate instructor,' recalled Taylor. 'And while we were here, he set me up with an agent.'

Enlisting the services of an agent was a vital step in getting Taylor noticed. Not only did it bring the benefit of all the agent's experience and contacts, but it also let directors and producers know that the hopeful applicant set before them was a serious proposition. Immediately, Taylor found he was busier than ever, 'There were more auditions. I heard "no", "no", "no", "no", so many times.' Fortunately, Taylor could draw upon the psychological discipline that was a cornerstone of his martial arts training. 'From karate, I had the confidence and drive to push myself,' he observed.

> I told my parents I didn't want to give up acting. And after weighing the good with bad, they agreed to move.'
> – Taylor Lautner

'My advice for people that want to act would definitely be, "You can't get down,"' asserted Taylor in an interview with Renata Joy of *Ultimatedisney.com*. 'Because the average booking rate when you're starting is one out of seventy-five auditions and that's *crazy*! So you can't just go to something and not get it, and get totally down and want to quit, because that's just not happening unless you're an extremely lucky and talented person. But, once you break into the business more, it will get better. You just can't get down and quit because it's very, very difficult.'

In addition to attending a seemingly unending procession of auditions, Taylor began taking weekly acting lessons, fighting not to fall behind in school and Mike's training sessions all the while. Ultimately, the strain of trying to keep to such a hectic schedule began to take its toll and Taylor decided that, in order to pursue a career as an actor, he would take a year out from competitive martial arts.

Fortunately, as the trial period neared its end, there came a sign that all of the hard work and sacrifice was beginning to pay off. 'I got one call-back,' recalled Taylor. 'That gave me the drive to keep going. It happened on our very last day there.'

Although the call-back didn't result in a role, more concrete progress was evident when Taylor scored a part in the 2001 feature film *Shadow Fury*. An action-packed tale of futuristic ninja clones, the film was directed by Makoto Yokoyama, who had been the stunt co-ordinator during Mike Chat's tenure in the *Power Rangers: Lightspeed Rescue* series. Yokoyama cast Taylor as Kismet, a cloned boy caught up in the battle between humans and clones, and he made his acting debut alongside movie veterans such as Sam Bottoms, who had featured in several major productions such as *Apocalypse Now* and *The Outlaw Josey Wales*.

Once studios began to show interest in Taylor, the move from Hudsonville to Los Angeles became permanent. 'It was a big deal to leave, all our family was here,' remembered Taylor. By 2002, the family had settled into life on the West Coast. 'Of course, we were all sad that our house was gone in Michigan,' he observed three years later. 'But it turned out for the best because we're having a lot of fun in California now.'

Taylor's next engagement saw his debut as a voice artist as he recorded a brief segment for an advertisement for *Rugrats Go Wild,* an animated feature that hit screens in 2003. Despite the limited nature of the role, Taylor was delighted. 'I was so ecstatic,' he admitted. 'I thought, "This is what I've been waiting for."'

Shortly after, Taylor experienced another first, cast for a minor role in Fox TV's *The Bernie Mac Show.* The series, which ran from 2001 to 2006, followed the trials and tribulations of a stand-up comedian suddenly required to care for his drug-addict sister's three needy children. Taylor's television debut came on 5 February 2003 – just six days before his eleventh birthday. The episode, titled 'Bernie Mac Rope-a-Dope', centred around the hapless Bernie and his wife attending a dinner party thrown by his boss and also featured a guest appearance from Wesley Snipes, best known for his big-screen appearances as Blade, the vampire slayer.

*Sitting pretty: Fresh-faced Taylor gets more than his recommended daily allowance at Camp Ronald McDonald's 2007 Halloween Carnival.*

Although Taylor's *Bernie Mac* appearance as 'Aaron' was little more than a walk-on role, it was a sign of just how far he'd come, and one to enhance his ever-growing résumé. In no danger of becoming complacent, however, Taylor resolved to give his chances of being cast another boost, seeking to broaden his range of talents further still. He took voice coaching and also began attending dance lessons.

Two thousand and three also saw Taylor make his return to the competitive martial arts arena. At an age where most kids would be taking their formative steps in serious sports, Taylor began his comeback, appearing as a founder member of Mike Chat's newly created six-strong XMA Performance Team. Appearing at such diverse events as the Orlando Sporting Goods Super Show, Oklahoma Sooners Basketball Half-Time Show, the MAIA Super Show in Las Vegas and the Big Five Sporting Goods Show in Los Angeles, Taylor's passion for martial arts was soon to be re-ignited.

In July, he won the World Junior Weapons title, which was broadcast on the ESPN sports channel, and by the end of the year he was ranked Number One in the world for his age by the North American Sport Karate Association for the disciplines of Black Belt Open Forms, Musical Weapons, Traditional Weapons and Traditional Forms.

Throughout Taylor's triumphant return to competitive martial arts, he kept attending auditions, and on Easter Sunday 2004 he appeared on *The Nick And Jessica Variety Hour,* a one-off special featuring husband-and-wife duo Nick Lachey and Jessica Simpson, harking back to sixties variety shows like *Sonny & Cher* and *Rowan & Martin's Laugh-In*. With a nice touch of post-modern irony, the show also featured appearances from Muppets Kermit the Frog and Miss Piggy, whose own show had, to an extent, parodied the song and sketch shows of yesteryear. Taylor appeared in several sketches and was particularly taken with Jessica Simpson, the singer-actress who shot to fame in hit reality show, *Newlyweds: Nick & Jessica*. Ever the gentleman, Taylor spoke in defence of his much-maligned co-star, insisting she's done nothing to deserve her ditzy, blonde reputation. 'That was lots of fun,' he observed. 'I got to meet her, she was nice. She wasn't stupid like everyone thinks she is.'

That same month, Taylor made a fleeting reappearance on national television with a small walk-on part in Warner's popular drama, *Summerland*. By coincidence, the plot of *Summerland*, like *The Bernie Mac Show*, hinged upon an adult suddenly charged with the care of three children – but that was where the similarities ended. Taylor's small role as a boy on the beach in an episode titled 'To Thine Self Be True' saw him appear alongside future *High School Musical 2* heartthrob Zac Efron, who featured as Cameron Bale in sixteen of *Summerland*'s twenty-four episodes.

> **'There were more auditions. I heard "no", "no", "no", "no", so many times.'**
> **– Taylor Lautner**

Two months later, Taylor reprised the role of Aaron for a second episode of *The Bernie Mac Show*. Entitled 'Being Bernie Mac', the show aired on 22 September. Shortly after, Taylor was back in another family-oriented sitcom: the Damon Wayans vehicle, *My Wife And Kids*. The plot of this series revolved around the timeless device of a generational battle between a patriarchal father (Wayans's Michael Kyle) who wanted a traditional family life, and his children, who had very different ideas. Taylor appeared in an episode called 'Class Reunion', which aired toward the end of the series' five-season run.

This time, Taylor's role was somewhat more substantial than had been the case with *The Bernie Mac Show* and *Summerland* – he played a bully named Tyrone who was picking on one of the Kyle kids. 'I got to be a bully and push this little kid around,' Taylor told *Kidzworld.com*. 'That was fun because I'm normally not a bully because my parents wouldn't allow me to do that. I'm just not that person, but it was fun to experience something new.'

By the end of 2004, Taylor had become a fixture on the Los Angeles casting scene. The experience built up through dozens of auditions had afforded him specific insights concerning the best ways to approach the process. 'When it comes to auditioning, I go through the script, go through the emotions that the writers want us to portray and we go through them and into the audition and meet with the casting director,' he told *eFilmCritic.com*'s Jason Whyte the following year. 'Sometimes, when it's really big and it's a feature film, we meet with our acting coach for about an hour and go over the scene.'

Even at this early stage of Taylor's acting career, the steady growth of his profile indicated that Dan and Deborah's decision to relocate their young family to California had been well founded. As his expanding résumé showed a steady progression, it was surely only a matter of time before Taylor landed his first major role.

*Taylor lights up the launch party for* Kewl *magazine, April 2007.*

# a bigger fish

# 3

'My dad says I can't date 'til I'm twenty-eight . . .
but I'm hoping to negotiate that one down.'
– Taylor Lautner

Taylor's strategy of widening his range of talents by taking acting lessons and voice coaching was proven to be a wise one when he was selected to voice the character of Youngblood in Nickelodeon's animated series *Danny Phantom*. The eponymous hero was a half-ghost, half-living boy who spent the series protecting his hometown from all manner of supernatural menaces, one of whom was Youngblood.

Initially portrayed as a comically malevolent pirate boy with a shape-shifting henchman, Youngblood re-appeared in several episodes of the series subsequent to his debut in 'Pirate Radio', which first aired on 22 July 2005. 'I've done three episodes so far and he's a lot of fun to voice,' Taylor explained to the *Oregon Herald*'s Mark Sells. 'Probably because I'm a kid-bully-pirate. I'm an evil ghost and a pirate and get to say stuff like, "Aaargh!"'

Youngblood proved to be a popular addition to *Danny Phantom*'s roster of supporting characters and re-appeared as a cowboy bent on driving Danny to distraction in an episode called 'The Fenton Menace', which hit screens in October. He made a further cameo as one of a group of ghosts who help save Christmas in the seasonally themed 'The Fright Before Christmas', before showing up again for a final time in series finale 'Phantom Planet', where he once again came to Danny's aid.

Taylor also lent his vocal talents to two episodes of the *Duck Dodgers* series – a show that re-cast classic Looney Tunes character Daffy Duck in the role of futuristic action hero, Buck Rodgers. He voiced an unnamed 'Terrible Obnoxious Boy' in the episode 'Good Duck Hunting', which aired on 7 October, and returned as the character Reggie Wasserstein in the following week's show 'A Lame Duck Mind'.

This was quickly followed by an encounter with one of Hanna-Barbera's classic stable of characters, as Taylor was hired for a couple of episodes of *What's New, Scooby Doo* – 'A Terrifying Round With A Menacing Metallic Clown', in which he provided the voice for a minor character named 'Ned', and 'Camp Comeoniwannascareya', which cast Taylor as a

*All the better to hear you: Taylor attends the
MTV Video Music Awards, September 2008.*

camper named Dennis.

Taylor also provided voices for a pair of short-lived projects, that of Silas, one half of *Silas And Brittany* – a dog and cat duo whose show aired on the Disney Channel – and a pilot for a projected series called *Which Way Is Up*, which would have seen him in the lead role of Orley, but failed to make it to the small screen. He was also hired to voice a string of radio ads that included Kellogg's Frosted Flakes and Legoland.

However, despite his blossoming career as a vocal talent, Taylor's main focus remained on becoming a screen actor. 'I definitely love film and live acting better than voiceover, but I do a lot of voiceover stuff and, you know what, I love both,' he told Renata Joy of *Ultimatedisney.com*. 'I like live acting and I love voiceover because you're not on camera and usually you're playing a person totally opposite of yourself and you just get to change your voice and be a weird character and that's an awful lot of fun.'

## 'He asked for a superhero pose and I did one of my martial arts moves.' – Taylor Lautner

Although the voiceover work continued to roll in – Taylor starred as the titular bully in the TV special, *He's A Bully, Charlie Brown* – a booking to appear in an episode of the romantic comedy series *Love, Inc.* represented a step in the right direction. The series followed the misadventures of a dating agency executive named Barry (played by Vince Vieluf, whose previous credits included *ER* and *Friends*) who is ironically struggling to find a suitable partner of his own. Taylor appeared in an episode called 'Arrested Development'. He played twelve-year-old Oliver, a boy desperate to win the affections of his first crush.

Since the move from Michigan some three years earlier, Taylor's progress had been encouraging and steady. He had accrued a solid résumé of film, TV and voice work and was becoming increasingly sought after by directors looking for an engaging, charismatic young actor for character roles. As is the case with most young actors, both he and his agent were continually looking for roles that would help develop Taylor's talents and raise his profile. This meant submitting to continual rounds of auditions and endless waiting for call-backs, a tiresome process that would prove overwhelmingly worthwhile when Taylor showed up to try out for a 3-D, CGI effects-laden family feature called *The Adventures Of Sharkboy And Lavagirl*. It was a role that would change his life.

Despite the radical impact that *Sharkboy And Lavagirl* was to have on Taylor's life and career, things got off to a slow start. 'The first audition was just with a casting director and they were like, "Okay, thanks Taylor! Bye!"' he recalled in an interview with *eFilmCritic. com*'s Jason Whyte.

'About two weeks later, we found out that Robert Rodriguez and his son, Racer [who came up with the idea for the film], wanted to meet with me at their hotel room in LA,' explained Taylor. 'So, I went down and met with them and did my scenes for the casting director and Robert. And then Robert took out his own video camera and wanted to tape me. He asked for a superhero pose and I did one of my martial arts moves.'

*Above: Aquatic antics: Taylor stars (alongside Taylor Dooley and Cayden Boyd) as the 'sullen, instinctual' Sharkboy in* The Adventures Of Sharkboy And Lavagirl *(2005). Below: Fortunately, the film's eerie underwater world was strictly computer generated.*

At that time Robert Rodriguez, who had carved out an impressive reputation directing such high-octane movies as *Desperado*, *From Dusk Till Dawn* and *Sin City*, was still unaware of Taylor's martial arts mastery. With an impromptu show from the young champion, however, that was about to change. 'I was there for quite some time. I was interacting with Racer Max for a while and Robert was filming tests with his video camera as well as getting several pictures,' Taylor recounted. 'I stood on one hand and I'm upside down and my legs are in a split position and his son really liked that. Unfortunately, LA was just the first spot that they stopped at before auditioning throughout the rest of the country. But fortunately, thousands of auditions later, they came back to me and told me I got the part.'

This represented a huge breakthrough for the young actor. A major feature, with a large budget, directed by a big-name filmmaker with a proven track record in making films for young audiences, such as the *Spy Kids* movies – it was precisely the chance Taylor had been waiting for, bringing guaranteed exposure and renown. The Lautners' reaction was appropriately hysterical. 'We freaked out,' Taylor told Terri Finch Hamilton of the *Grand Rapids Press*. 'My whole family couldn't sleep for, like, a week.'

> 'We freaked out. My whole family couldn't sleep for, like, a week.'
> – Taylor Lautner

In fact, Robert Rodriguez was not only offering Taylor his first big break, but an equally rare opportunity to put his creative capabilities to the test, fleshing out Sharkboy's personality beyond what was written. 'Usually you get breakdowns and it says what your character is like and Robert Rodriguez just wanted us to create our own characters,' Taylor explained. 'He didn't want to put anything on a breakdown. So when you see the breakdown, it says, "Create your own." I just thought that Sharkboy would be whatever I wanted him to be, and I did that, and I guess Robert liked it.

'Sharkboy is very self-confident and sometimes he gets way, way too confident and that's what starts wars in the film, and he was separated from his father when he was very young,' observed Taylor. 'He is also very jealous of Max [the human character who creates Sharkboy and Lavagirl] because Lavagirl is very over-motherly to Max, so Sharkboy doesn't really take that well. He's very acrobatic, he shoots water out of his hands . . . he's pretty fun. His personality is quite a bit different from my own.'

Revealingly, the young heartthrob cited a sense of humour with bite as one of the main qualities he brought to the role. 'I'm very sarcastic like Sharkboy, I think,' Taylor mused. 'A line that I have in the movie that's totally me is when our Train of Thought crashes into the mountain in the Land of Milk and Cookies and we land on the giant cookie, and Max is like, "Sharkboy, what happens when your train of thought wrecks?" And I'm like, "Well, can't be good, buddy." I thought that was totally me.'

Not only did Robert encourage Taylor to imbue Sharkboy with facets of his own personality, he was equally keen for the martial arts champ to show off his moves. 'When I went in to meet with Robert, he didn't know that I did martial arts,' he told *RadioFree.com*'s Michael J. Lee. 'And then he saw a DVD of me while we were shooting, and he asked me to choreograph my own fight scene. So I just did my stuff and he picked his favourite stuff I did, and he just added in the plug hounds that I fought. And it was cool. I had no clue I was going to be doing that.'

The character of Sharkboy was essentially a superhero in the mould of a junior version of Marvel's Sub-Mariner, or DC's Aquaman. This was ideal for Taylor as he remains a huge fan of the medium. 'I love watching the *Spider-Man* movies. Although he's probably not my favourite superhero, I love watching the movies. As for a super power, I like x-ray vision, like Superman, who can see right through things. I think that's pretty cool.'

Taylor's interest in superheroes was a fascination that stayed with him, as he explained to *Vanity Fair* journalist Adrienne Gaffney in November 2008. 'My favourite movie is *Iron Man.* I tell people that I think it's just as good as *Dark Knight,* if not better, and people tell me I'm crazy. I really like *Iron Man.*'

Certainly, *Sharkboy*'s plot gave Taylor, who understood the dramatic dynamics of superhero fiction, plenty to work with. 'It's about a ten-year-old named Max who doesn't fit in well in school,' he explained. 'He gets picked on by bullies. And one day he dreams up two superheroes, Sharkboy and Lavagirl, while daydreaming in class. Eventually, Sharkboy and Lavagirl become real and they need Max to help them save their home world, a world which Max created. It's under destruction and being destroyed by Mr Electric.'

Like Marvel's Sub-Mariner, Sharkboy was orphaned and left to grow up in an undersea realm. 'When he was younger, about five years old, he was separated from his father in a storm,' recounted Taylor. 'His father was a marine biologist and after his father disappeared, he was all alone . . . except for the sharks. Raised by sharks, he became very self-confident. And he winds up being half-boy, half-shark, occasionally going into these shark frenzies.

'I just thought that Sharkboy would be whatever I wanted him to be, and I did that, and I guess Robert liked it.'
– Taylor Lautner

'He was fun to play because he got to do a lot of acrobatic stuff. And he gets to move like a shark and throw lots and lots of temper tantrums,' Taylor declared. 'He starts biting and ripping stuff. He gets really, really crazy. And that's when you don't want to be near him.'

Playing Lavagirl to Taylor's Sharkboy was Taylor Dooley, a twelve-year-old actress making her professional debut having recently narrowly missed out on the part of Samantha Parkington in *Samantha: An American Girl Holiday* – a television adaptation of Valerie Tripp's popular *American Girl* series of children's books.

Taylor Dooley was also originally from Michigan and the two Taylors immediately found a remarkable amount of common ground. 'It's really weird,' Lautner asserted. 'Our moms have the same name, we both have younger siblings, and we live practically across the street from each other in LA. If I were to drive to her house, it would take only take seconds.'

Unsurprisingly, given their uncannily similar backgrounds and the male Taylor's relaxed and easygoing nature, the two quickly became firm friends. 'We go out to dinner together and we have many of our friends from the set over for sleepovers,' he revealed.

Both Taylors also got along famously with another of their co-stars, eleven-year-old Cayden Boyd, who had already appeared in a number of movies including the 2004 remake of *Freaky Friday* and *Dodgeball: A True Underdog Story*. Cayden would subsequently go on to use the superhero expertise he acquired through playing Sharkboy and Lavagirl's creator, Max, by appearing as the young Angel in the third instalment of the *X-Men* series of films. 'We had a lot of fun on the set with Cayden. After we were done shooting, the three of us would go behind the set and play hide and seek and climb trees,' recalled Taylor Lautner. 'And we all see each other a lot since we live only a few blocks from one another.'

Like Taylor Lautner, Cayden was a huge sports fan and consequently came in for a fair share of teasing about his support of the Texas A&M University sports teams, who are often referred to by their nickname of 'Aggie'. 'We played jokes on Cayden all the time,' admitted Taylor. 'You see, he's a big Aggie fan and we were shooting on the University of Texas campus. And of course, UT and Texas A&M have a huge rivalry. So, we'd have lots of fun with him. There was a dog on the set named Tippy and we'd put UT stickers and a UT collar on her and would say that it was UT's new mascot. We also went back and forth, posting different messages and stuff on our doors.'

'My least favourite part was the three hours of school on the set every day. School is good, but it's not really fun.'
– Taylor Lautner

Indeed, Taylor's outgoing personality was ideally suited to life on a set that he described as 'a very family-friendly environment'. 'My favourite part of being in a movie is because you get to meet a lot of nice people and you get good relationships from that and it's a lot of fun to meet those new people,' he observed.

For three months, *The Adventures Of Sharkboy And Lavagirl*'s tight filming schedule cut into the time available to Taylor for his martial arts practice. 'I still train at my house, but I can't compete because it's just way too busy,' he explained.

However, the studio was obliged to ensure that the young cast kept up with their education – which, although absolutely non-negotiable, wasn't always to Taylor's liking. 'My least favourite part was the three hours of school on the set every day. School is good, but it's not really fun,' he grinned. 'You gotta do school three hours a day and sometimes more because they want to bank hours. At the end of the movie, if you don't have enough time or if you want to relax more, you're going to be leaving in a couple of days, then you get to use some of your bank hours. That's pretty much how it works.'

Although attending lessons between shoots was a drag, Taylor's positive outlook ensured that he saw the upside of the situation. 'It's okay, 'cause you do have those other kids with you unless you're the only kid in the movie.'

As well as making friends and hanging out with his co-stars, Taylor was delighted to have the opportunity to work with a director of Robert Rodriguez's calibre. 'I was definitely familiar with the *Spy Kids* movies 'cause I loved all three of them and I watched them a lot. And my mom heard a lot of great stuff about him, so when I booked the movie and I heard

I got to work with him, I was really excited. And when we got there, I saw why, because he was so much fun to work with,' Taylor declared. 'Everybody loved working with him. He played video games with us on the set. For instance, while I'd be shooting a particular scene, he'd be off playing video games with Taylor [Dooley]. It was so much fun.'

In particular, Rodriguez's 'hands on' approach to filmmaking helped to set the young actor at his ease. 'Most directors are like, "Get your work done, and go home. Do this, this, this, this, this and goodbye. We'll see you tomorrow." Robert will be with us during breaks and even after shooting. He would take us out on his boat from time to time. I'm used to football and karate coaches yelling all of the time for whatever reason, and Robert will not do anything like that. He was great to be around.'

Similarly, the director's lack of ego and understated style provided Taylor with an excellent example of how to handle success without becoming arrogant or self-important.

Twilight *tease: In an episode of MTV* Spoilers, *swooning members of Team Jacob were treated to more than just a sneak preview of the vampire romance.*

'He's very, very humble and he never lets anything get to his head. He's like a star director, but then he wears cowboy hats and jeans with holes in them all the time, so we all love him.

'What's so amazing about Robert is that he directs his films, he writes them, he edits them, and he's even the cameraman,' asserted Taylor. Though the down-to-earth director's most impressive accomplishment came as something of a surprise: 'Best of all, he's a terrific pizza maker. He makes the best pizza! In his house, he has this big, stone oven. It's about fifteen feet tall and he makes the most incredible pizza and ravioli.'

'I like 3-D movies. It gets the audience more in the moment. You feel like you're actually there with them.'
– Taylor Lautner

Aside from the junior members of the *Sharkboy And Lavagirl* cast, Robert Rodriguez's company included such seasoned performers as comedian, DJ, and actor George Lopez and *Scream* star David Arquette. But, despite the formidable experience they brought to the project, Lautner revealed that these talented professionals still knew how to have fun on set. 'George Lopez was great,' he beamed. 'We talked a lot with him. He's a really nice guy and he's a lot of fun to be around. You can see on the DVD that came out two days ago that he's playing paper a lot of times with us. He's throwing papers at us and hiding behind his desk and we're throwing them at him. He was really fun to be around.

'As for David Arquette, we didn't get to see him that much because while he was on the set, we were in school,' Taylor recalled. 'For the most part, he seemed very, very quiet. And very, very nice, always cracking jokes on the set. While the jokes would go along with the individual scenes, nobody would be able to stop laughing and they'd always have to start over.'

Recreating the crazed, Technicolor world of *Sharkboy And Lavagirl* on screen required a significant amount of special effects, which presented specific challenges for Taylor and the rest of the cast. 'Ninety percent of it was done on green screen,' explained Taylor. 'We just had three days at a house, three days at a school, and that was about it. And we had one day at a playground. All the other fifty-five days were on the green screen.'

> 'What's so amazing about Robert is that he directs his films, he writes them, he edits them, and he's even the cameraman. Best of all, he's a terrific pizza maker. He makes the best pizza!'
> – Taylor Lautner

The 'green screen' technique chosen by Rodriguez involves filming actors in front of a plain, single-colour backdrop (usually green, but sometimes blue). Later on, a separate set of images are overlaid on the background presented by the blank screen. By means of this visual trick, actors can appear to be flying, under the sea – in any imaginable setting at all, without the expense or danger associated with filming there for real. Of course, this was an entirely new experience for Taylor. 'It was my first time working on a green screen; and there's just *nothing* around, it's all green screen. You have to interact really carefully with your actors, because that's the only thing that is real. You really have to have a good imagination, and Robert helped us a lot with that. He would be really specific about the actions that we would have to make and what would appear behind us. He made many sketches and drawings of the surroundings.'

Certainly, Taylor sometimes found the process of using green screen technology to be a surreal experience. 'I'd say the first two weeks were kind of difficult,' he admitted. 'On the screen, you see like "big ol' shark boat with turbo boosters", and I'm just on this green box with two little green handles.'

The movie was also shot in 3-D, which, like the green screen, required specific acting techniques. 'The 3-D stuff you have to make your body different so the 3-D works,' Taylor explained to *About.com*'s Rebecca Murray. 'Like if you were holding something, you'd put your hand in front of the camera so it sticks out at the audience. But then when you get really in the moment, you want to move your body but you can't. It's difficult but it's fun.'

Despite the difficulties involved in shooting in 3-D, Taylor benefited greatly from the help and advice provided by Robert Rodriguez, and quickly mastered the necessary skills. 'Sometimes, when something is supposed to be in 3-D, like when I hold my Sharkboy Palm Pilot right in the camera so it's sticking out at the audience, you have to keep your hand really still so it's not shaking. Or else, the audience is always shaking and they don't like that,' he explained. 'You just got to stay in one place for the 3-D.'

On the whole, Taylor found that the process proved worthwhile and declared himself a fan of the three-dimensional medium. 'I like 3-D movies. It gets the audience more in the moment. You feel like you're actually there with them. I think it's more fun to do it 3-D.'

'Whenever I get mad, I go into a shark frenzy, and then I have the teeth. And when it's like a half-shark frenzy, I only have the bottoms. And then sometimes they fell out. And one time I like choked on it. They make you look ugly, man! They were really cool, but ugly at the same time.'
– Taylor Lautner

The other technical aspect of *Sharkboy And Lavagirl* that was new to Taylor involved the costumes – previously, the young actor had only been required to wear everyday outfits for roles, so squeezing into a superhero outfit represented something of a novel departure for him. 'It definitely takes a lot more time,' he observed. 'I was in the hair and make-up trailer for, like, forty-five minutes every day and then wardrobe for a half-hour. I had to get my whole suit on and everything. It was definitely a lot longer to get ready for Sharkboy because I'm playing a superhero. For Sharkboy, it's kind of harder to be in the moment because he's a superhero, and I'm not really a superhero. It was pretty easy, but playing a normal kid in real life is a lot easier.'

'My suit was all made of a urethane rubbery thing,' recalled Taylor Dooley. 'He [Lautner] had separate parts that he could connect and unconnect, but mine was just one big chunk of urethane. So it was kind of heavy in the very beginning, but I got used to it. And it looks really uncomfortable, but it was really comfortable, actually.'

To complete the Sharkboy look, Taylor was also required to wear a specially constructed set of prosthetic fangs. 'Whenever I get mad, I go into a shark frenzy, and then I have the teeth. And when it's like a half-shark frenzy, I only have the bottoms. It's like rubber and they just stick it in,' he explained. 'They like stick it in the top and the bottom. And then sometimes they fell out. And one time I like choked on it. They make you look ugly, man! They have like three layers. They were really cool, but ugly at the same time.'

Taylor found that he was on more familiar territory when it came to the physical aspects of the filming process, which enabled him to draw upon his martial arts training. '[Robert Rodriguez] saw a tape of me and he let me choreograph my own stunt scene in the film. I also do a song and I flip to that.'

However, even someone as physically fit as Taylor found some aspects of the *Sharkboy* shoot exhausting. 'They had me on wires and I'm running on a treadmill and it's like going ninety-nine miles an hour. And it's really tiring because they had me do that for ten minutes straight. Sometimes you just want to go, "Stop!"' Despite the effort required, Taylor insisted that he enjoyed the whole experience of being suspended in mid-air during shots. 'The wire work was one of our favourite parts just because you got to hang in the air upside down and all that kind of stuff.'

Both Taylors entered into the spirit of the filming process with enthusiasm and found the whole experience rewarding. There were also plenty of opportunities to have fun with certain scenes. 'One of them is when we're on the giant cookie and I got to step in a big puddle of chocolate and then I got to eat it. And I also liked getting whipped cream and ice cream all over us 'cause that was fun,' Lautner recalled. 'It was real chocolate and then the ice cream was actually just coloured whipped cream. Because we land on the cake and there's supposed to be frosting and ice cream and we got whipped cream on us.'

The movie presented its young cast with the chance to learn more about the filmmaking process, develop as actors and experience many new things. The one of these that caused Taylor Dooley the most trepidation was the thought of shooting her first screen kiss. 'I was really nervous and I was always telling the hair and make-up guy how nervous I was. It was only a peck on the cheek, but I was really nervous about it,' she admitted.

> 'They had me on wires and I'm running on a treadmill and it's like going ninety-nine miles an hour. Sometimes you just want to go, "Stop!"'
> – Taylor Lautner

Of course, the rest of the company saw Taylor's anxiety as a golden opportunity to have some fun with the young actress. Taylor made the mistake of telling Robert Rodriguez that it would be her first such scene and from that moment, her fate was sealed. 'Right before the kiss, he goes, "Sharkboy off set, we're going to do the kiss. Bring in the stand-in,"' she recalled. 'So they bring in this wooden post that is wrapped with green tape, and he goes, "Kiss it like you're kissing Sharkboy." So I don't know what's going on, and I'm kissing this piece of wood. I do it maybe two times, and he goes, "Okay, a little more, a little longer." And then I go to do it a fourth time, and he starts cracking up. And then the whole set starts cracking up. Everybody knew about it.'

Making *The Adventures Of Sharkboy And Lavagirl* took Taylor Lautner's nascent acting career to a new level. The young actor had learned a lot, had immense fun and completed his first major feature. He had assimilated an entirely new set of skills, gaining crucial on-set experience that would serve him well in the future. Soon enough, Taylor would be facing the next challenge of his screen career, dealing with life as a rising young star, known and loved by a mass of feverish fans.

*Va-va-voom! Taylor's presence adds a certain something to the opening of the luxurious Malibu branch of John Varvatos, October 2008.*

# fantastic life

'I just thought it was so cool. I couldn't believe
people wanted my picture.'
– Taylor Lautner

Once filming for *The Adventures Of Sharkboy And Lavagirl* was complete, Taylor soon found that the release of the film that featured him in his first starring role would bring with it a succession of new experiences.

The first of these was the film's Los Angeles premiere in June 2005. 'Previously, I'd done the red carpet five times before, attending the premieres of *Sahara*, *Sisterhood Of The Travelling Pants*, and *Ladder 49*,' Taylor explained to *Oregon Herald* reporter Mark Sells. 'But walking the red carpet, you wouldn't believe how many photographers are there; "Taylor, turn over here. Turn to the right. Hold it here. To the left. Now over here." It's really crazy on the red carpet, but knowing that it was *your* premiere made it even more fun.'

Taylor had found making the film so enjoyable that he later admitted that seeing the completed movie made him feel slightly wistful. 'The first time I saw it was at a cast and crew screening. It wasn't as different as I thought it would be. But it was fun watching how much fun we had on the set and how it turned out as a movie. It made me think of all the memories and moments from all the different scenes we shot.'

Although the happy days on set were now in the past, the movie would have an enduring effect on the young actor's outlook. 'I love being able to play characters that are nothing like you, like Sharkboy, and becoming them,' asserted Taylor. 'It's also getting to meet new people like Robert Rodriguez and actors and the relationships that are made from meeting those people that is very rewarding.'

*The Adventures Of Sharkboy And Lavagirl* received a wealth of positive reviews. Writing in the *Los Angeles Times*, Carina Chocano asserted that, 'Lautner and Dooley are compelling as the sullen, instinctual Sharkboy and the radiant, hot-headed Lavagirl, and it's easy to see why they dominate shy, hesitant Max's dreams.' *Variety*'s Joe Leydon was equally enthusiastic, describing the movie as 'a spirited romp guaranteed to engross

*Saintly supporter: Taylor attends* Variety's Power of Youth *auction,
held in October 2008, in aid of crucial research at St Jude's Children's Hospital.*

even the most attention-deficient pre-teens. Performances by the three young leads are winningly sincere and unaffected.'

The film went on to gross just under $40 million in the US alone – $12 million in the first weekend of its release. It was also nominated for an Imagen Foundation Award for Best Movie, while Robert Rodriguez was nominated for Best Director. Excitingly, both Taylors were nominated for the 2006 Young Artist Awards for Best Performance in a Feature Film (Comedy or Drama) – Leading Young Actor and Actress.

The sheer number of people who had turned out to see *Sharkboy And Lavagirl* guaranteed that Taylor could no longer count on being an unknown face in the crowd. 'Ten-year-old boys were the ones who first recognised me,' he recalled in an interview with Terri Finch Hamilton of the *Grand Rapids Press.* 'I'd be in the store, and boys would whisper to their moms. Then the moms would say, "Excuse me – are you Sharkboy?"'

Taylor's profile was raised further by having his likeness appear on all manner of Sharkboy merchandise. 'We were just in an Old Navy and they have these Sharkboy and Lavagirl T-shirts that they're selling, and one kid kept staring at me and the sticker pack that he just received with my picture on it,' he grinned. 'That was really funny, having the kid go, "Oh my gosh! You're the *real* Sharkboy! One sec, I have to go tell my friend," and he runs over, grabs him and we talk for a few minutes.'

'It was fun watching how much fun we had on the set and how it turned out as a movie. It made me think of all the memories and moments from all the different scenes we shot.'
– Taylor Lautner

Although Taylor's friendly and outgoing nature ensured that he was ideally suited to cope with recognition from fans, there were still situations that caught him by surprise. 'I've had an action figure before and it was weird,' he declared in an interview with *canmag.com*'s Fred Topel. 'They had action figures at McDonald's and Target. It was definitely weird. We have a couple. We have a couple saved because you never knew that it would happen again.'

The idea that the success of *Sharkboy And Lavagirl* would be transitory combined with Taylor's customary unaffected outlook to make certain that there was little chance of this first taste of fame going to the young star's head. At school, he was the same regular kid his friends had always known. 'Kids still looked at me as Taylor, because they knew me from before,' he recalled. Though still in his teens, Taylor is a young star with the maturity to realise that 'you gotta remember who your friends were before you got famous'. He quickly learned to be wary of people who 'suddenly want to be your best friend'.

The negative aspects of fame aside, Taylor was delighted to discover there were plenty of people out there who'd seen *The Adventures Of Sharkboy And Lavagirl*, enjoyed the movie and his performance in it, and wanted to know more about the young star and where to look out for him next. In other words, Taylor was beginning to acquire a fanbase.

*Left: Twilighters – Team Jacob needs you! Taylor begins amassing an army of devoted followers at* The Adventures Of Sharkboy And Lavagirl *premiere in June 2005.* ***Right:*** *Natural-born showman: Taylor flips for the crowds at the same event.*

In order to satisfy this interest he arranged for an official website to be established – *taylorlautner.com*. 'We post messages and put up new pictures for wherever we go, so it's a good way to keep a diary of what we do,' Taylor explained. 'There's also a contact page where you can email me – I try to respond to every email we get – and there's a PO Box for autographs. We're just keeping things updated and plan to keep it that way.'

The site received plenty of hits and there was a steady stream of fans emailing Taylor for further information, autographs and pictures. 'We usually get about twenty a day,' he revealed. 'My visits about a month ago was about one hundred to two hundred hits, but since it's closer to the *Sharkboy*, we recently had over three thousand visits.'

With Taylor's popularity on the rise, resting on the laurels of *The Adventures Of Sharkboy And Lavagirl*'s success was never an option for the driven young star. Miramax held an option to cast him in any sequel, so there was a possibility that he might be called on to reprise his performance should the circumstances be right, but Taylor knew better than to pin all of his hopes on this outside chance. 'Dimension and Robert will decide if they want to do any more,' he shrugged, philosophical as ever on the subject of Sharkboy's future. 'I guess we'll see how well the film does and go from there.'

In fact, where Taylor went from there was directly to Toronto, to begin shooting *Cheaper By The Dozen 2*. As its title implies, the movie was a sequel continuing the

*Bring it! Taylor as one of the competitive Murtaugh clan in* Cheaper By The Dozen 2 *(2005).*

'Kids still looked at me as Taylor, because they knew me from before. You gotta remember who your friends were before you got famous.'
– Taylor Lautner

comedic misadventures of the large and unstable Baker family, headed by veteran actor Steve Martin. 'There's the huge Steve Martin family on vacation, and then I play one of the kids in the competing family,' explained Taylor. 'Carmen Electra plays my mom and Eugene Levy my dad, in a family full of athletes and straight-A students. I have seven brothers and sisters, and we have competitions and wars with the Steve Martin family.'

Although Taylor's role as Eliot Murtaugh was far smaller than that of Sharkboy, the movie offered him further opportunities to develop as an actor working alongside such well-known stars as Carmen Electra (best known for her appearances in *Baywatch*), Eugene Levy – who played Mitch Cohen in the hilarious 2003 satire of folk music, *A Mighty Wind* – and daytime television host Bonnie Hunt.

The majority of Taylor's scenes were filmed during the summer at Stoney Lake in Burleigh Falls, Ontario, and the large number of kids playing Baker or Murtaugh offspring ensured that the shoot had a holiday camp atmosphere. 'We canoe ride and we're doing a bunch of activities and competitions,' announced Taylor. 'We also get to live in a cabin on the lake for four weeks, so that's going to be a riot.'

Taylor quickly adapted to having so many established actors around him. 'That's when I stopped looking at movie stars as movie stars, and just looked at them as people,' he observed. He got on particularly well with Alyson Stoner, a twelve-year-old actress and dancer who was reprising her role as Sarah Baker from the first film and would go on to star in Disney's *Camp Rock* movie series.

*Cheaper By The Dozen 2* was released on 21 December 2005, and although the critics gave the movie largely negative reviews, much of the media opprobrium was directed at the perennially unfunny Steve Martin. 'Martin seems like he's performing in a straitjacket, playing everything cute and precious,' observed *Seattle Post-Intelligencer* reviewer Sean Axmaker. More positively, *Variety*'s Justin Chang noted that 'in the most engaging subplot, tomboyish Sarah Baker (Alyson Stoner) develops a crush on Eliot Murtaugh (Taylor Lautner, of *The Adventures Of Sharkboy And Lavagirl in 3-D*)'.

> 'That's when I stopped looking at movie stars as movie stars, and just looked at them as people.'
> – Taylor Lautner

The movie grossed around $90 million from US and UK box-office takings alone, which once again represented a significant level of exposure for Taylor, who noticed that the number of people who recognised him had tripled after *Cheaper By The Dozen 2*. 'But now, it was girls,' he grinned.

Two thousand and five can be viewed as the year in which Taylor nailed his ambitions to acting rather than any of the myriad career options he could have chosen to pursue instead. The making of *The Adventures Of Sharkboy And Lavagirl* and *Cheaper By The Dozen 2* had dominated Taylor's time for much of the year and necessitated that the young actor make some tough choices. 'I don't compete nationally for martial arts anymore, but I still train at my house to keep up the skill,' he told *RadioFree.com*'s Michael J. Lee. 'For my dancing, I really don't do that anymore because I'm so busy with my other things in life. I was unable to even do football this year in school. When I did, the day went something like this: get down to school for football practice, drive to an audition *while* doing my homework, drive *back* to football practice, drive home at about 8:00-8:30, eat dinner and go to bed. That was really busy but now it's just acting and school.

'I played football my whole life and had to give it up last year because I had to miss too many practices and it was kind of rough for me,' lamented Taylor. 'It is kind of hard watching the high-school football games now. I played running back and slot receiver, and strong safety on defence.'

Although it was a wrench for him to give up competitive martial arts, Taylor found it easy to name the branch of performing he enjoyed best of all. 'Definitely acting,' he declared. 'Yeah, by far. Dancing – I don't really do anymore because I'm way too busy. Same with karate, because you have a tournament once a month, where you got to miss a weekend for that. And you also gotta be training two hours a day. Karate is just a horrible mix with acting. So I had to pick either karate or acting, and I picked acting.'

Despite his withdrawal from competitive sport, Taylor never lost touch with Mike Chat and still found time to keep up with the latest developments across the XMA scene. 'I still try and keep up with it when I can in my free time,' he told *About.com*'s Rebecca Murray. 'I go down to the XMA headquarters in North Hollywood where my karate trainer just opened up this big complex and it's awesome. It's top notch. So I do go down there when I can and try and kick off some rust.'

Taylor's busy schedule allowed him little time for relaxation, as he explained to *eFilmCritic.com*'s Jason Whyte: 'I don't really have time for that. I haven't had that in a long time. If I did, I'd go over to a friend's house and play video games or something.'

Such was Taylor's focus on acting, cinema and movie-making that he used what little spare time he did manage to grab to hone his skills, while having fun at the same time. 'I make movies with my sister, Taylor Dooley and her brother all the time,' he revealed. 'We're making one right now with my video camera and my stills camera, and it's a lot of fun. We have credits and music that we edit on the computer.'

'You're performing for people, you're performing for audiences. You can't be boring. You can't bore them.'
– Taylor Lautner

One of Taylor's home-produced features was titled *The Ladynappers*, and featured Taylor Dooley's younger brother Drew in the title role, with his sister as his victim. Taylor cast himself as the heroic CIA agent charged with rescuing the unfortunate Miss Dooley, and there was even a role for Makena as 'Goth Girl' – a street-smart character who helps her brother track down Dooley's damsel in distress. 'It's a combination of action and comedy and it's just a lot of fun to make,' explained the young auteur. 'We were making one like that when we were down in Austin, Texas filming *Sharkboy* and Robert Rodriguez's wife Elizabeth told us that if we could finish it, maybe we could put it on the DVD, but we never finished it.'

Taylor may have been faced with a frantic schedule that gave him very little in the way of free time, but his acting career was developing beyond all expectations. Thanks to the support of his parents and his innate drive and discipline, Taylor was becoming increasingly aware of the dynamics of his chosen craft and precisely what would be required to reach the top. 'You're performing for people, you're performing for audiences. You can't be boring. You can't bore them,' he insisted. 'My dad always says this: "You can't just *do* it, you've got to *perform* it." 'Cause if you just go up there and *do* it then people are just going to be watching you and be like, "Ah, he's pretty good." But if you go up there and *perform* it, they're gonna wanna watch you and keep watching you.'

Within a few short months, Taylor would be amazed by just how many people wanted to keep on watching him.

*Back in black: Taylor smoulders for the camera at the
Kari Feinstein Golden Globes Style Lounge, January 2009.*

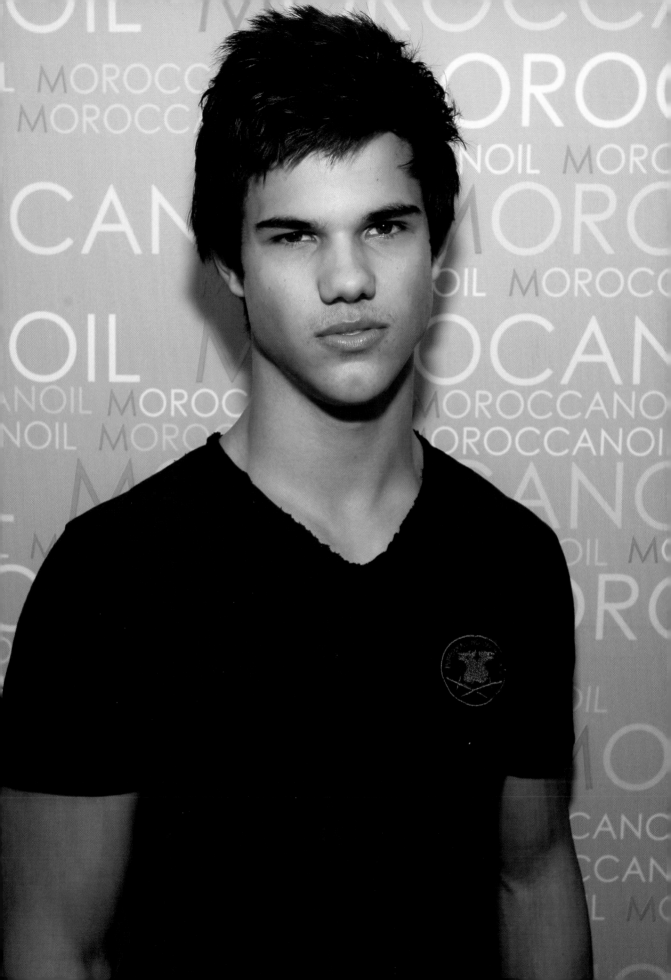

# scary 5 stories

'I'm just thankful to be doing what I'm doing.
It's unreal. I'm just so excited to be doing this.'
– Taylor Lautner

In November 2007, Taylor received a call from his agent urging him to audition for a forthcoming movie based upon a book that he'd never heard of. The film was called *Twilight* and, while that left Taylor none the wiser, his agent seemed tremendously excited by the opportunity and all that it could mean for his client.

'When I first found out I had an audition for some *Twilight* movie, my agent told me, he's like, "Yeah, this one's kind of big. This one's big." And I was like, "I've never heard of it,"' Taylor told Rebecca Murray of *About.com*. 'So I go in on it, and yeah, the director's really cool. I meet the director, I go back and I read with Kristen Stewart and she's really cool. Still have no idea what the project is about or how big it is.'

'They needed sides for me to read,' Taylor explained to *buddytv.com*'s Kim Wetter, 'so they used the beach scene from the movie, from the script, and then I had two other scenes and they literally just pulled quotes from *New Moon* and *Eclipse* and made them sides. So I actually got to do a couple of scenes from *New Moon* and *Eclipse* with Kristen. It was kind of fun. It was a little taste.'

All Taylor really knew was that he had auditioned for the part of a teenage werewolf named Jacob Black and that the hopefuls had been narrowed down to a shortlist of three actors potentially in line for the role – one of whom was himself. His curiosity duly piqued, the young star got online to look up *Twilight*. 'I realised how big it was,' he told *Grand Rapids Press* journalist Terri Finch Hamilton. 'Suddenly, it was all over the internet. I started hearing about all the hype, all the fans. I thought, "Oh my goodness. If I get this, it'll be huge." I realised I really want this.'

A month after the auditions, the call from the studio came through – he'd got the part. 'I was sweating, I was so excited,' recalled Taylor. 'I'm just, "Oh my gosh, what am I getting myself into?" This is life-changing, so now I'm so excited to be a part of it.'

Taylor's excitement was well founded. Originally published in 2005, Stephenie Meyer's

*Taylor attends Access Hollywood's Bertolli Oven Bake Meals,*
*staged in January 2009 as part of the Golden Globe celebrations.*

debut novel shot into the Top Ten of the *New York Times* bestseller list within a month of its release as a hardback. *Twilight* went on to spend ninety-one weeks on the list, eventually selling seventeen million copies worldwide, having been translated into thirty-seven languages. Praised by the *Times* for capturing 'perfectly the teenage feeling of sexual tension and alienation', the dark tale of forbidden romance, beguiling vampires and teen angst proved a massive hit with young audiences at a time when attracting teenagers to literature was proving increasingly difficult.

At the time of Taylor's audition for the role of Jacob, Meyer had written two sequels to *Twilight*: *New Moon*, which appeared the following year, and *Eclipse*, which was published in August 2007. Subsequently, a fourth instalment of the saga, *Breaking Dawn*, hit bookstores in August 2008.

Hardly surprisingly, given the way in which he was kept permanently busy with acting, martial arts and schoolwork, Taylor was not a big reader. 'I've never been a book reader,' he admitted. 'Very rarely, maybe an occasional school book.' This changed with *Twilight*.

Once he had been cast as Jacob, Taylor immediately consumed the first novel of the series. 'I was not a vampire or werewolf fan at all,' he admitted to *Interview* magazine's Michael Martin. 'I auditioned for the role, and as soon as I got it, I started reading the books. I'm not a reader, but I really did get hooked on them.'

'I auditioned for the role, and as soon as I got it, I started reading the books. I'm not a reader, but I really did get hooked on them.'
– Taylor Lautner

'I think with *Twilight*, the whole series, there's a bit of everything in it – there's romance, there's action-adventure, there's like a little horror in it, there's everything,' observed Taylor in an interview with *Reelzchannel.com*'s Naibe Reynoso. 'So, I think that's why it attracts so many people, because it's a little mix of everything.'

Having read the novel and discovered just how many others shared his love of the story, Taylor was thrilled to be given the chance to become a part of what was already a globally popular fantasy. 'As soon as I was cast, that was when I found out how big this was and what the potential was,' he recalled. 'I was so excited to be a part of it. I was like, "Wow." Originally I was just excited to work with Catherine Hardwicke and I did a chemistry read with Kristen Stewart and so I was excited to work with them. But then, when I found out how much of a phenomenon this was, it was crazy for me.'

Of course, scoring a role on such a high-profile project alongside the likes of director Hardwicke (who at that time was best known for directing such movies as *Thirteen* and *Lords Of Dogtown*) and Stewart (who shot to fame on account of her remarkable performance opposite Jodie Foster in 2002's *Panic Room*) brought its own attendant pressures. 'I was kinda nervous about it at first,' confessed Taylor. 'When I was on the plane flying out there, I was like, "How's this going to be?" But it was great. Everybody was so fun to work with.'

Having read *Twilight* and immersed himself in the heightened emotion of Stephenie Meyer's world, Taylor developed an intuitive understanding of Jacob Black's character. 'He's very interesting. I love the way Stephenie wrote him,' declared Taylor. 'He's a Native

*Taylor flashes his trademark smile in front of a crowd of snap-happy young fans at the MuchMusic Video Awards in Toronto, Canada.*

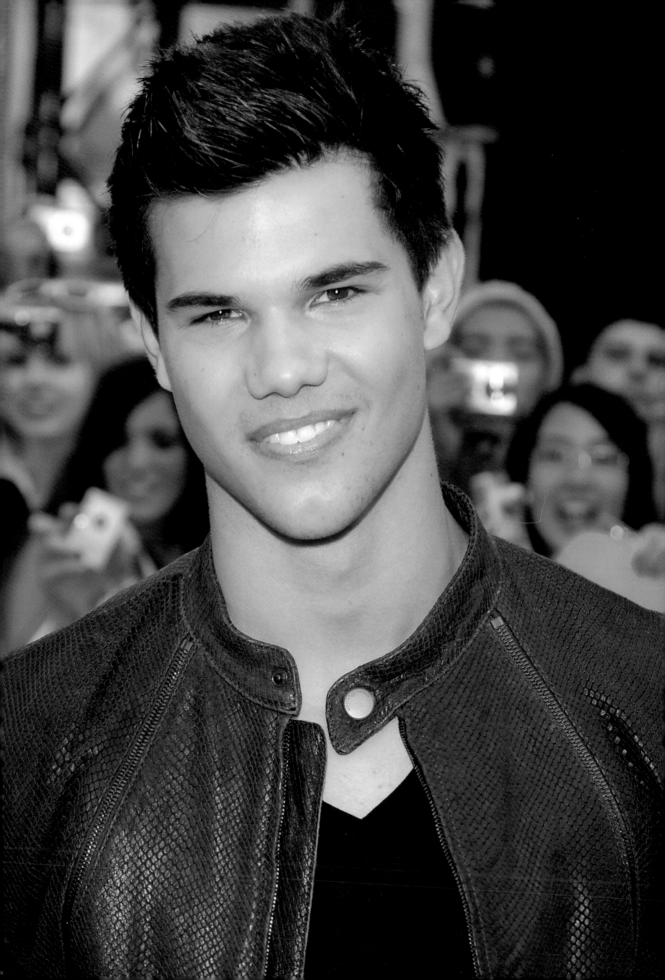

*Taylor and his* Twilight *co-stars Robert Pattinson, Cam Gigandet and Kristen Stewart get to grips with each other at the 2008 MTV Music Video Awards.*

'I like to think I am more Jacob's human side. I enjoy people. I really like people. I like to think I am friendly. But I also love Jacob's werewolf side as well because it challenges me as an actor.'
– Taylor Lautner

American. He's very friendly, and easy to talk with, then in the second one it becomes interesting because he turns into a werewolf. And what I find cool is, like, he has this Native American side who's just this happy-go-lucky kid, then he has this werewolf side where he's trying to hold back his temper and he wants to be violent.'

'I'm not a vampire – I'm just a boy,' Taylor explained to *acedmagazine.com*'s John Delia. 'My character is Jacob Black and he is very good friends with Bella. They were very good friends when they were kids and then she moved away to Phoenix and now in *Twilight* she is back to Forks, has grown up quite a bit, and Jacob has a huge crush on her. He is actually the one who spills the beans to her about her cute little love Edward being a vampire.

'Jacob is a really interesting character because he definitely feels like an outsider [. . .] he doesn't go to the same school as everybody else, he's on the reservation,' recounted Taylor. 'But Bella brings him out of that. Also, Jacob brings Bella out of this huge depression she's in. She wants to kill herself, she's so sad. Jacob is her sun. He brings her alive, out of this deep hole.'

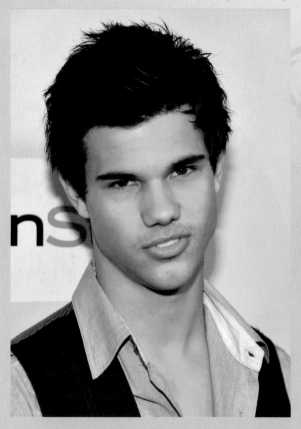

In style: Taylor arrives at the HPFA Salute to Young Hollywood Party, held at the Nobu restaurant in Los Angeles, December 2008.

As had been the case with the slightly sarcastic Sharkboy, Taylor perceived a little of his own personality in Jacob's character. 'I like to think I am more Jacob's human side,' he mused. 'I enjoy people. I really like people. I like to think I am friendly. But I also love Jacob's werewolf side as well because it challenges me as an actor. It challenges me because his human side is completely opposite to his werewolf side. One second he's like the nicest guy on earth, then he goes werewolf on you and he's grumpy all the time and Bella is like, "Wow, what happened to you?"'

In order to fully assimilate the role, Taylor reasoned that he'd need to get to grips with Jacob's Native American heritage. 'Before I even started filming *Twilight*, I studied up on all of the Quileute tribes and legends and myths and everything about them,' Taylor explained in an interview with *Metronews. ca*'s Tania Soghomonian. 'When I got up to Portland, Oregon to film, I was able to meet with about ten Quileute tribal members. I got to talk to them and what I really learned is that they're not much different than me, and that was very unexpected.'

'They showed up in basketball uniforms,' Taylor revealed to *MediaBlvd.com*'s Christina Radish. 'Somehow, we got on the topic of what they like to do for fun, and they go to the beach and check out girls.'

'I interviewed them and just wanted to get to know them,' Taylor told MTV's Larry Carroll. 'One thing they do that I noticed is they don't need to be told to what to do. If the trash is getting full, they empty it out. They're always helping each other. They're always there for each other. So I just want to make sure I can bring that part of Jacob alive.'

The Quileute are a tribe of some seven hundred and fifty people who settled where the Quillayute River meets the Pacific Ocean in Clallam County, Washington. Renowned for their skill as builders and craftsmen, they made their living on the tumultuous grey waves, constructing sturdy wooden fishing vessels for whaling. Originally a deeply spiritual people, many Quileute beliefs have been sadly lost in the years since Europeans came to dominate the continent.

Yet, with Stephenie Meyer's *Twilight Saga*, the line between fact and fiction begins to blur; in her world, a handful of imposing tribesmen, ambiguously known as the 'protectors' of Forks forest, share a secret. They're not just teen tearaways, but vampire-battling lycanthropes, capable of shifting shape whenever they choose. For this pack of towering, muscle-bound teens, there's nothing mythical about the werewolf – it's a powerful legacy coming true every moonlit night of their lives. And, as the other kids in Forks agonise over prom night, calculus and college, Jacob is struggling with a private horror of his own; the realisation that, whether he likes it or not, he'll soon be one of the pack.

Besides Bella's best friend, Meyer's books feature a small community of other intriguing tribe members, including Jacob's father Billy (played in the movie by former bodybuilding champion Gil Birmingham), Leah and Seth Clearwater (who, in *New Moon*, undergo the same chilling transformation as Jacob), Quil Ateara (played in *New Moon* by young actor Tyson Houseman), Sam Uley and Embry Call (both cited simply in the film's credits as 'Jacob's friend'). Incidentally, *Twilight* was not the first time the Quileute had appeared in popular fiction, having inspired Susan Sharpe's novel, *Spirit Quest*, back in 1991 – proving that the rich history of this tribe has lost none of its power to fascinate.

Taylor's own quest to bring authenticity to his portrayal of Jacob was aided by regular discussions with Stephenie Meyer. 'It's really cool because she comes up here every once in a while for her favourite scenes,' he explained. 'At the beginning of filming, she gives a list of her favourite scenes that she wants to be up here for. You've got the best person in the world to ask for advice. So if you have a question, you can just walk on over and ask her.'

One of the aspects of the character that fascinated Taylor most was the bipolar disparity between Jacob's open and engaging Native American traits and the savage beast within.

'One second he's like the nicest guy on earth, then he goes werewolf on you and he's grumpy all the time and Bella is like, "Wow, what happened to you?"' – Taylor Lautner

'He is very friendly and outgoing. He loves Bella and is very loyal to Bella and his dad. But on the werewolf side, they're very fierce and just attacking, and they have this huge temper. So there's a lot of stress and things going on inside him as he's trying to keep his temper to himself. I love that part, which Stephenie created, with the contrast between the Native American side and the werewolf side of him.'

Additionally, it transpired that Taylor has some Native American heritage of his own. 'Actually, I am part-Native American,' he revealed. 'We learned that through [preparing for] this film. I'm French, Dutch and German, and on my mother's side, she has some Potawatomi and Ottawa Indian in her.'

It's possible Taylor has these genes to thank for the dusky complexion that made him an ideal fit for the role of a Quileute boy. 'I'm not really sure where I get the dark, tan skin from. It just kind of happened,' he observed. However, in order to replicate Jacob's long, dark hair, Taylor was required to wear a wig. 'The costume and wardrobe were the easiest part,' he recalled in an interview with *Vanity Fair*'s Adrienne Gaffney. 'The most difficult part for me was the wig. It took a while to put on and take off.'

'When I first heard that I was going to be wearing a wig I was really excited. I was like, "Cool, I have never worn a wig before, this is going to be fun, change my look up a bit,"' Taylor told *Teen* magazine's Mario Chavez. 'But then, after the first day of filming I was through with it. It was really itchy; it was always getting in my face! I'd be trying to eat

*'It was really itchy,' Taylor said of the wig he had to wear while filming* Twilight, *'it was always getting in my face!'*

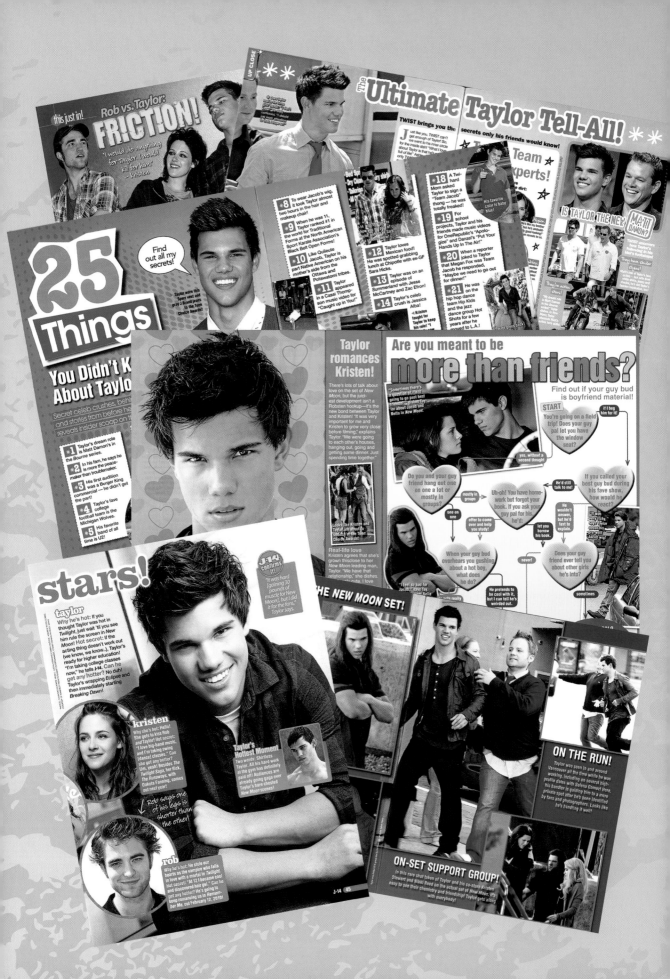

## Rob vs. Taylor: FRICT!ON!

"I would do anything for Taylor. I would kill for him!" —Kristen

## The Ultimate Taylor Tell-All! **

**TWIST brings you the** secrets only his friends would know!

Just like you, TWIST can't get enough of Taylor! So, we went to his inner circle for the inside dish! "What I love about Taylor is that he's full of life," Asia only TWIST!

### Team Experts!

**dirt!**

His favorite color is baby blue!

## IS TAYLOR THE NEW MATT DAMON?

# 25 Things

## You Didn't K
## About Taylor

Secret celeb crushes, behin and stories from before he reveals insider scoop on th

Find out all my secrets!

Taylor wore this Sper vest and gray in the Team Choice Awards!

*1 Taylor's dream role is Matt Damon's in the Bourne series.

*2 In his fam, he says he is more the peace-maker than troublemaker.

*3 His first audition was a Burger King commercial — he didn't get the part!

*4 Taylor's fave college football team is the Michigan Wolves.

*5 His favorite band of all time is U2!

*8 To wear Jacob's wig, it took Taylor almost two hours in the hair and makeup chair!

*9 When he was 11, Taylor ranked #1 in the world for the Traditional Forms at the North American Sport Karate Association's Black Belt Open Forms!

*10 Like Quileute Jacob, Taylor is part Native American on his mother's side from the Ottawa and Potawatomi tribes.

*11 Taylor appeared in a Cassie Thomp-son music video for "Caught up in You!"

*12 Taylor loves Mexican food! He was spotted grabbing lunch at Chipotle with ex-GF Sara Hicks.

*13 Taylor was on an episode of Summerland with Jesse McCartney and Zac Efron!

*14 Taylor's celeb crush is Jessica Alba!

*18 A Twi-hard Mom asked Taylor to sign a "Team Jacob" thong — he was totally freaked!

*19 For school projects, Taylor and his friends made music videos for OneRepublic's "Apolo-gize" and Danze's "Put Your Hands Up In The Air!"

*20 When a reporter joked to Taylor that Megan Fox was Team Jacob he responded. "Maybe we need to go out for dinner!"

*21 He was on the hip hop dance team Hip Kids and the jazz dance group Hot Shots for a few years before he moved to L.A.!

### Taylor romances Kristen!

There's lots of talk about love on the set of New Moon, but the juici-est development isn't a Robsten hookup—it's the new bond between Taylor and Kristen! "It was very important for me and Kristen to grow very close before filming," explains Taylor. "We were going to each other's houses, hanging out, going and getting some dinner. Just spending time together."

**J-14 Confirms it!**

Looks like Kristen and Taylor are about to cozy up at the Teen Choice Awards!

**Real-life love**
Kristen agrees that she's grown thisclose to her New Moon leading man, Taylor. "We have that relationship," she dishes. "He's so cute. I love

## Are you meant to be
# more than friends?

Find out if your guy bud is boyfriend material!

**START**
You're going on a field trip! Does your guy pal let you have the window seat?

if I beg him for it!

yes, without a second thought

Do you and your guy friend hang out one on one a lot or mostly in groups?

Uh-oh! You have home-work but forgot your book. If you ask your guy pal for his he'd:

If you called your best guy bud during his fave show, how would he react?

mostly in groups

He'd still talk to me!

one on one

offer to come over and help you study!

He wouldn't answer, but he'd text to explain.

let you borrow his book.

When your guy bud overhears you gushing about a hot boy, what does he do?

never!

Does your guy friend ever tell you about other girls he's into?

He pretends to be cool with it, but I can tell he's weirded out.

sometimes

"I feel so bad for Jacob," says Tay for about Jacob and Bella in New Moon.

# stars!

## taylor
Why he's hot: If you thought Taylor was hot in Twilight, just wait 'til you see him rule the screen in New Moon! Hot secret: If the acting thing doesn't work out (we know, we know...), Taylor's ready for higher education! "I'm taking college classes now," he tells J-14. Can he get any hotter? No duh! Taylor's wrapping Eclipse and then immediately starting Breaking Dawn!

"It was hard [gaining 30 pounds of muscle for New Moon,] but I did it for the fans," Taylor says.

## kristen
Why she's hot: Hello! She gets to kiss Rob and Taylor Hot secret: "I love big-band music and I'm taking swing [dance] classes." Can she get any hotter? Um, yeah! Besides the Twilight Saga, her flick, The Runaways, and Dakota Fanning, comes out next year!

**Taylor's Hottest Moment**
Two words: Shirtless Taylor. All his hard work at the gym has definitely paid off! Audiences are already going gaga over Taylor's bare chested New Moon scenes!

Rob says one of his legs is shorter than the other!

## rob
Why he's hot: He stole our hearts as the vampire who falls in love with a mortal in Twilight. Hot secret: "At 12 I became cool and discovered hair gel." Can he get any hotter? He's good romancing us in Remem-ber Me, out February 12, 2010!

# THE NEW MOON SET!

## ON THE RUN!
Taylor was seen in and around Vancouver all the time while he was working. Including on several high-profile dates with Selena Gomez! Here, his handler is guiding him to a more private spot after he's been identified by fans and photographers. Looks like he's handling it well!

## ON-SET SUPPORT GROUP!
In this rare shot taken of Taylor and his co-stars Kristen Stewart and Nikki Reed on the actual set of New Moon, it's easy to see their chemistry and friendship! Taylor gets along with everybody!

lunch and it's in my mouth and, yeah, even when were filming the scenes and I'm talking and it's in my mouth and argh!'

Certainly, Taylor was in no hurry to make long hair part of his everyday look. 'I just don't think I could stand walking around like that in public,' he insisted. 'I don't know. It's so weird looking at myself in the mirror and going, "Is that me?" It's like it looks so different, it's weird to me. It's like, "Wow!" I've never had my hair longer than it is right now, so just looking at myself like that is like, "Wow, do I look like a girl? I do look like a girl, ah!"'

Taylor did find that the one small advantage of having to wear the long, black, itchy wig was that it provided some protection against the inclement climate on the Portland set. 'I filmed a scene on the beach with my wannabe girlfriend and wardrobe had originally just picked out jeans and a T-shirt for us and we got there and there was sleet, hail, it was pouring rain, freezing cold forty-mile-per-hour winds, the tide was up to our knees,' Taylor explained. 'It was insane. We filmed the whole thing that way and we ended up wearing several pairs of socks, a couple of pairs of jeans, sweatshirts, ponchos, beanies, mittens . . . everything. After each take we would crowd into this little tent around the heater and have our cup of hot chocolate and try to warm ourselves up before the next shot.'

'This is going to sound weird, but the beach scene was my favourite scene. It was painful. I was hating it but at the same time, looking back at it, it was a lot of fun finishing every take and huddling over a little heater, and having our hot chocolate to warm us up. It was my least favourite and my favourite.'
– Taylor Lautner

'We looked like little sissies,' added Edi Gathegi (best known for his portrayal of Dr Jeffrey 'Big Love' Cole in the TV series *House*), who played vampire Laurent in both *Twilight* and *New Moon*. 'It's always cute when you could see any of the vampires being all fierce, and then huddled with hot chocolate,' teased Rachelle Lefevre – who took the part of murderous vamp Victoria.

'The thing I thought was interesting about the weather was that, usually on film sets, when it starts raining they have to call cut and wait for the rain to stop,' observed Taylor. 'But, for *Twilight*, it was the opposite. I did an interview under a tent and literally, while they were filming, this girl was in high heels and the wind blows and the tent comes up and flies over our heads and she falls down.

'We did every scene, every angle, everything with the hideous weather up until about 2:00pm. Then the sun randomly appears and it stops raining and they say, "Let's do everything again." So we do everything again, and sure enough they use the nice weather in the film.'

Paradoxically, despite the discomforts involved in filming in the face of a blizzard, Taylor would nominate the beach scene as his favourite moment from shooting *Twilight*. 'This is going to sound weird, but the beach scene was my favourite scene. It was painful,' he recalled. 'I was hating it but at the same time, looking back at it, it was a lot of fun finishing every take and huddling over a little heater, and having our hot chocolate to warm us up. It was my least favourite *and* my favourite.'

At just sixteen, Taylor was the youngest person on the *Twilight* set. For most actors, arriving to film a new movie and meet the cast can be nerve-wracking enough, but Taylor's youth and relative inexperience meant that he was very much the 'new boy'. Fortunately, the on-set atmosphere was friendly and he was quickly made to feel at home. 'I was a little nervous at first,' admitted Taylor. 'But no, it was great . . . Everybody's really nice and easy to relate to. The cast really had great chemistry and we all hung out. We're all really good friends now, so that's really cool.'

Taylor got on particularly well with Kristen Stewart, who played Jacob's (and Edward's) love interest, Bella Swan. 'Kristen's awesome! She's an amazing actress and she's an awesome girl. She's a lot of fun,' he declared. 'The whole cast is really close. It would be difficult for our characters if we weren't. It's a love triangle, and we need to understand each other. So the fact that we're close and can talk things through in rehearsals, and if we're out at dinner, we'll just randomly start talking about the scene we're shooting the next day . . . If we weren't able to do those things, I don't know where we'd be.'

> 'Edward? Who's Edward? Is there an Edward character in the book?'
> – Taylor Lautner

Although the cast got along famously, relations between Bella, Jacob and Edward (played by British heartthrob Robert Pattinson) could hardly be so straightforward, with Jacob and Edward in constant competition for the affections of accident-prone Bella. This conflict has filtered down to the *Twi*-fans themselves, who remain split between Team Edward and Team Jacob. For every fan girl swooning over Edward Cullen's brooding vamp, there's another convinced that snarling sweetheart Jacob Black is the only boy for Miss Swan. In contrast with her conflicted character Bella, Kristen Stewart has stated who she's siding with in no uncertain terms. Pulling Taylor close on stage at 2009's Comic-Con, she told a reporter for *E! Online*, 'Read into this.' And Jacob's undying devotion to Bella, whether she returns his love or not, is surely enough to make any member of Team Edward think again.

'Edward? Who's Edward? Is there an Edward character in the book?' joked Taylor. 'In the first movie, Jacob's hot, but Jacob won't live forever. You have people that say that it's cool to live forever, but he's more human-like than Edward. With the first movie, and the first book, you don't really know much. You just know that he's this really happy-go-lucky guy, who is just in love with Bella.

'Bella, she's just young. She doesn't know what she's thinking right now but she'll realise it some time. Personally, I don't get the vampire thing. They're cold; werewolves are hot. I mean, cold, hot – come on! And I think Bella is just confused at the moment. She doesn't know what's best for her and the Team Edward fans, but they'll come around. They'll come around.'

The levels of partisan support between the competing Edward and Jacob camps clearly demonstrates the way in which *The Twilight Saga* has captured the public imagination, with many readers agonising over Bella's dilemma as if it were their own. The devotion of those fans who've pledged themselves to Team Jacob is something that's never ceased to amaze and delight the modest young star. 'I was surprised. There are a lot more than I expected. It's awesome. I love just diving into the crowd and giving them hugs. It's fun.'

Although Taylor's role in *Twilight* is significantly smaller than in *New Moon*, he features in several memorable scenes – one of which required him to drive Bella's notoriously hard-to-handle truck. As a newly qualified driver, Taylor approached the task with a wise degree of caution, arriving on set early to demonstrate his capabilities to the producers. 'I've got my license in my back pocket to show them I'm okay and that I won't kill them . . . hopefully,' he laughed. 'I'm going to test out driving Bella's truck and my family's truck. One of them is an automatic, so that will be nice and easy. The other one has no power steering, so I'll have to muscle it. That will be interesting. I've never done that before . . . I'm going to be driving with my [real-life] dad right next to me, and that should be interesting. We want to make sure I get used to it, so it looks natural.'

*Taylor shields himself from the chilly Vancouver weather in-between takes whilst shooting scenes for* New Moon.

In addition to getting used to Bella's beat-up old truck, Taylor also took time out to master pushing Gil Birmingham around in Billy Black's wheelchair. 'I've got to get used to my dad's wheelchair, so that [pushing it] looks very natural, like I've always done this my whole life,' he explained.

After filming on *Twilight* had been completed, Taylor was recalled to shoot the prom scene, which wasn't originally in the script. 'When I read the script I was like, "Really, he doesn't come to the prom?"' he recalled. 'I think I asked Catherine [Hardwicke] about it and I forget what she said. But I was just like, "Oh, okay . . ." But sure enough, you know, they were like, "Okay, we're doing it."'

> 'It's awesome. I love just diving into the crowd and giving them hugs. It's fun.'
> – Taylor Lautner

Like most movie adaptations of popular novels, the differences between the two mediums required a variety of alterations to Stephenie Meyer's original story in order to make it fit the cinematic format. However, Taylor firmly believes the movie stays faithful to both the style and content of the book – losing none of the swooning, hormonal lyricism that made it so special. 'I felt that they did an amazing job, taking the parts needed and putting them in the script. I think the exciting part, for the fans, is just seeing their book brought to life, on the big screen, and seeing what their characters look like. They have this pre-set image of what the characters look like, so I think it's going to be interesting for them to see what we look like.

'I think it is so close that if you like the books then you are going to love the movie. The books are pretty successful and I think the fans are going to be pretty proud.'

> 'I think it is so close that if you like the books then you are going to love the movie . . . The fans are going to be pretty proud.'
> – Taylor Lautner

'Stephenie Meyer was a consultant,' explained Edi Gathegi. 'The people love her story and she's stamping it with her approval. It's so cool that they gave her that opportunity. I'm sure she wouldn't have done it without that. She was on set a lot.' 'And she had a cameo on the film,' added Rachelle Lefevre (eagle-eyed *Twi*-fans will no doubt have glimpsed Meyer ordering a vegetarian sandwich in one diner scene, just a few tables away from where Charlie is mustering up the courage to ask Bella if she likes any of the boys in town). 'Real fans will know when it's her and freak out. She was so critical of herself too. She's rightfully proud of the books that she's written, so to see her being nervous about being on camera was so funny.'

'Obviously you have to condense almost six hundred pages to a one-hundred-page script, but I think they did the best job possible of taking a book and making it into a two-hour film,' Taylor surmised. Besides, he felt sure the close-knit atmosphere on the set would eventually shine through with the finished film. 'We all get along really well and I think definitely our chemistry off screen is going to be transferred on screen.'

As *Twilight*'s 17 November 2008 release date drew closer, Taylor was convinced the film had the kind of universal appeal that would ensure that it became a huge hit. 'All of the fans can relate to the characters. I mean, a lot of our fans are in high school so they can relate,' he told *teamsugar.com*. 'The other thing is it's a romance. The girls love the romance. But it's not only a romance – it's an action romance. So I think the movie is for everyone. It's got romance, action, horror – it's got everything.'

Similarly, Taylor was quick to refute any suggestion that the romantic nature of *Twilight* meant that it was a movie for female audiences only. 'The film is amazing and it is not just a romance. One of them just happens to be a vampire, and it adds a lot to it. It is very dangerous. It is a life or death situation. The whole second half of the movie is non-stop action,' he asserted. 'I know that all my guy friends would totally love the film.'

As the excitement around the movie's release intensified to fever pitch, it became apparent Taylor had not exaggerated the extraordinary appeal of *Twilight* in the slightest.

*So it is written: Taylor signs autographs for fans at Twilight's **world premiere in Los Angeles, November 2008.***

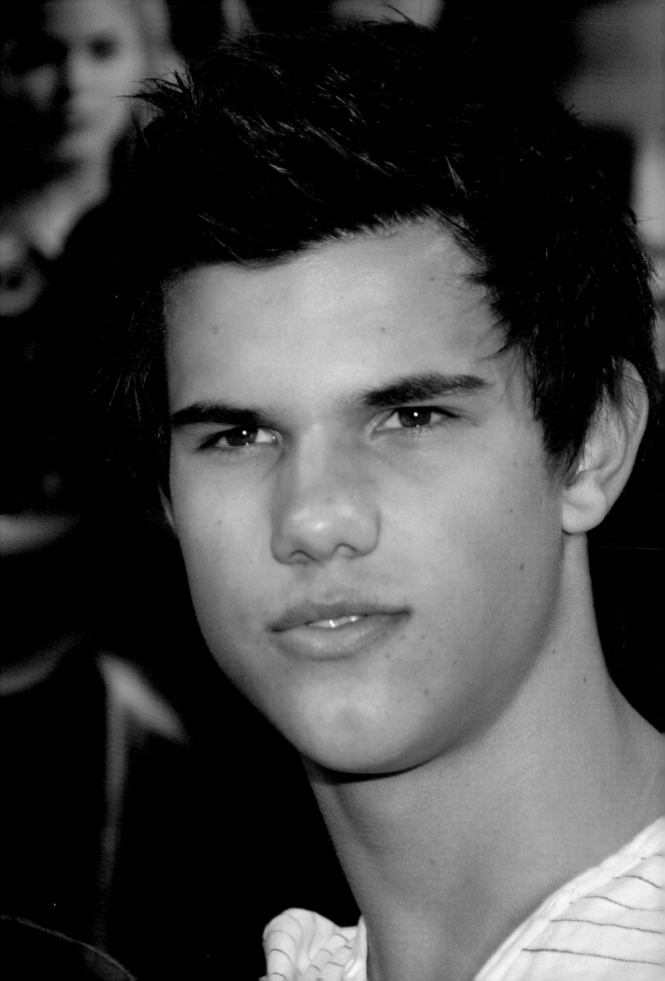

# twilight supernova

'It's weird to see my character's name
on other people's bodies.'
– Taylor Lautner

With just a fortnight to go before *Twilight* hit cinemas across the USA, Taylor and his co-stars headed out on a publicity tour to meet and greet expectant fans. Such was the level of interest in the forthcoming movie that the cast quickly discovered that they were locked into a punishing schedule.

'The next two weeks are going to be the busiest weeks of my life,' an excited Taylor declared to *About.com*'s Rebecca Murray. 'This whole weekend is press junkets until Sunday night, Monday morning I wake up, get on a plane and do a six-city tour in six days throughout the United States. Come back at midnight on the sixteenth, the next day is the seventeenth – the premiere. A couple of days later it comes out.'

Although Taylor's internet research had provided him with some impression of the fans' ardent passion for Stephenie Meyer's novels, it could hardly have prepared him for the intensity of the hysteria that he encountered on the road. 'They are very intense, but it's cool that they're so dedicated and so passionate,' he told *Interview* magazine's Michael Martin. 'So I'm thankful for the fans. I like meeting them. But, yeah, they're pretty intense. Sometimes it becomes a little overwhelming.'

Indeed, Taylor later admitted to *canmag.com*'s Fred Topel that the response of certain fans left him somewhat taken aback. 'It's very surprising, but at the same time, it's because the fans behind it are just extraordinary. The fans are driving this thing, and the storyline's awesome. It's got everything in it, so it's going to be interesting to see on the big screen.'

With expectations for the coming movie approaching fever pitch, Taylor confessed to feeling a certain amount of pressure, charged as he was with the responsibility of bringing Meyer's beloved character to life on the big screen. Visualised by readers everywhere, he was painfully aware of all that Jacob Black meant to the *Twi*-fans; would his performance live up to the fantasy? 'Sometimes it can be nerve-wracking. It's hard not to be nervous when you know there's a few million fans out there who are just dying for this movie

*Brooding for the cameras during a question-and-answer session
with the rest of the* Twilight *cast at a Los Angeles Hot Topic store.*

*A call to arms: Taylor unwittingly gives fans a glimpse of that famous physique.*

to come out and making sure it's top notch, the best, and the characters are wonderful. So I mean yes, it gets nerve-wracking sometimes. But for the most part I'm just really excited. I'm totally stoked to be a part of it.'

Despite the global furore, Taylor refused to let the fan-worship go to his head, preferring to point to Stephenie Meyer's character as the source of the excitement. Characteristically modest, he shrugged off his heartthrob status, observing: 'We're just lucky enough to be a part of this. I don't think it has much to do with me personally; it's more because I'm playing the beloved Jacob Black.'

The pre-release publicity tour wasn't the first time that Taylor had experienced the undying devotion of Twilighters everywhere. His introduction to their powerful infatuation with the series had come a couple of months earlier, when he attended the July 2008 San Diego Comic-Con International. Founded as a comic-book convention in 1970, the Comic-Con has expanded over the years to encompass a wide range of popular culture, from movies and video games to action figures. By 2008, the event had become so popular that it was only possible to attend by purchasing a four-day pass in advance. These sold out at breakneck speed, with scalped tickets changing hands for many times their face value. It was the perfect place to preview *Twilight* and hold a panel discussion with the cast.

On the day it seemed as if all of the one hundred and twenty thousand ticket-holders were trying to pack into the six-thousand-five-hundred-capacity auditorium at once. 'There were eleven thousand people waiting in line for autographs,' recalled an amazed Taylor, who spent several hours signing books and pictures, in between giving a host of TV, radio and web interviews. 'Comic-Con was crazy. I knew it was going to be. They had told me, "This is a big event and there's going to be, like, six thousand fans there." We got there and it was huge. Just coming out on stage and hearing everyone scream and seeing how many people were in that auditorium was crazy.'

The following month, Taylor was caught up in more fan madness when he attended a

*Signing autographs, inciting screams, and breaking hearts – all in a day's work for the eligible young Mr Lautner.*

midnight release party for *Breaking Dawn*, the final instalment of the *Twilight* series. The event took place at a branch of Barnes & Noble situated in the RiverTown Crossings mall in Grandville, Michigan. As Taylor was in the area visiting friends and family, he decided that it would be fun to look in on the party. As soon as he entered the store he was mobbed, as fans recognised him and cried, 'That's Jacob Black!'

'They're so dedicated and so passionate. So I'm thankful for the fans. I like meeting them. But, yeah, they're pretty intense. Sometimes it becomes a little overwhelming.' – Taylor Lautner

'Then I heard this mom say, "No, that kid's name is Taylor. He used to live across the street from me." And the girls said, "No, that's Jacob Black." And the mom said, "No, that's Taylor – he's my old neighbour,"' he recounted in an interview with Terri Finch Hamilton of the *Grand Rapids Press*. 'She didn't know I was gonna be in the movie.'

Once Taylor had explained to his former neighbour why he was getting mobbed in a local bookstore, the young star spent the next two hours chatting and signing autographs for anyone who'd made the effort to come out, finally leaving the store after 2:00am. 'I didn't realise a thousand girls were gonna be there,' he explained. 'I would feel miserable if I left and there were still a hundred girls who had been waiting two hours to get my autograph.'

*Grin and bear it: Taylor at the* Twilight *premiere – embracing his inner wolf, or simply squinting at the incessant camera flashes?*

Naturally, things are always more extreme on the internet, and if the face-to-face fan passion had left Taylor a little surprised, what he found online sent him into a state akin to shocked disbelief. 'I'm not online crazy twenty-four-seven but I run across things sometimes. It's weird. It's weird to see shirts that say "Team Taylor" on them and other articles of clothing,' he observed.

'One of the other weirdest fan things is somebody sent me a link and said, "What is this?" And it was a picture of women's underwear being sold online with "Taylor" written on it,' he revealed to *Vanity Fair*'s Adrienne Gaffney. 'So it was kind of weird to have women's underwear with my name imprinted on the front.'

> 'I did [growl once], but it was extremely embarrassing so I never did it again!'
> – Taylor Lautner

Although Taylor joked about not having the thong, there were plenty of people who went online and ordered one. 'There was some middle-aged woman. She's like, "Guess what Taylor? I'm wearing the Team Taylor panties!"' recalled Taylor. 'I'm like, "No way." And she's like, "Would you mind signing them?" And luckily my publicist was right there and she's like, "We've got to go do an interview." And I'm like, "Okay, yeah, I'll think about that one."'

*Robert Pattinson, Kristen Stewart and Taylor spread the* Twilight *gospel around the world at the film's Tokyo premiere in February 2009.*

Taylor encountered a more restrained mode of mature appreciation from the *Twilight* Moms, a group of older female readers who loved Stephenie Meyer's novels and gathered around a website set up by Lisa Hansen as a hobby which grew to occupying her time for around thirty hours a week. 'I felt like the only one out there my age who was completely obsessed with these books and that there was something severely wrong with me,' she recalled. After finding out that she was most assuredly not alone, Lisa set up a MySpace group linked to *Twilight* and the *Twilight* Moms were born. Her site, which can be found at *twilightmoms.com*, is now enormously popular and offers its own interviews, merchandise and updates.

'The *Twilight* Moms were actually on set while I was filming one of the scenes, and they were definitely fun. It was one of the most exciting interviews I've had. They're so passionate about this book,' Taylor told *MediaBlvd* magazine's Christina Radish. 'What the *Twilight* Moms do,' added Edi Gathegi, 'which is fantastic for our careers, whenever there is something else that we are doing they will put that on everyone else's radar and then the *Twilight* fans will come and support our other work.'

> 'We're just lucky enough to be a part of this. I don't think it has much to do with me personally; it's more because I'm playing the beloved Jacob Black.'
> – Taylor Lautner

'People are always, like, *Twilight*? Is that teenage chick-flick book? No, it is not,' insisted Taylor in an interview with *acedmagazine.com*'s John Delia. 'And the *Twilight* Moms are just as crazy about it as they are. It is insane, but they are so supportive . . . Our fans are incredibly supportive. I don't think there are better fans out there.'

Certainly, Taylor's experiences ahead of *Twilight*'s premiere clearly illustrated the point that fans of the novels come in all ages, shapes, sizes and personality types. 'We've met many different fans: the criers, who come around quite often; the hyperventilators who stop breathing and have to have a medic come,' he recalled. 'We've definitely seen some passion.'

Regardless of all the adulation, both online and in person, Taylor remained as determined as ever to hold on to some sense of perspective. 'I try not to pay attention to it,' he admitted. 'I'm no different than anybody else.' He also had the advantage of Dan and Deborah's constant support, making sure that the pressures of fame didn't go to the young star's head. 'My parents wouldn't allow it,' insisted Taylor. 'That's not the way they brought me up.'

'We want to protect him,' asserted Dan. 'Because of all that's happening for him, we want him to do normal things. We kept him in public school as long as we could, so he could be with his peers. We give him responsibilities at home – chores he has to do. He gets an allotted allowance and he has to budget it.'

With his parents squarely behind him, there's little chance of Taylor developing any kind of over-inflated ego. He regularly returns to Grand Rapids, where it is apparent that, despite his success, he's the same Taylor that everyone there remembers from just a few short years ago. 'He signs autographs for all the kids, poses for pictures. He's still that well-

*Fang versus claw: Robert Pattinson as Edward Cullen and Taylor Lautner as Jacob Black.*

'I would feel miserable if I left and there were still a hundred girls
who had been waiting two hours to get my autograph.'
– Taylor Lautner

mannered, great kid,' confirmed Tom Fabiano. 'There was one mom here, a big *Twilight*
fan, and when I told her Taylor was gonna stop in she screamed, "I have to meet him!"'

Further evidence of Taylor's unaffected nature came on the night of the *Twilight*
premiere, a frenzied affair that took place amid hordes of screaming fans in Westwood,
Los Angeles. While those in attendance were described by MTV's Larry Carroll as a 'who's
who of young Hollywood', Taylor typically thought of his family rather than his public
image when the time came to choose who would accompany him to the glitzy event. 'I'm
having one of my grandparents come out for the movie and they're actually going to the
premiere,' he told *Teen* magazine's Mario Chavez. 'All of my family lives in Michigan and
every family member has read the books, I mean all four of my grandparents, aunts, and
uncles, everybody! It's just crazy cool that they love it so much.'

Screenings of *Twilight* weren't the only place fans could catch Taylor in action in the fall of
2008. After the movie wrapped he spent two days a week shooting *My Own Worst Enemy*,
a series starring former Hollywood bad boy Christian Slater as deep-cover secret agent

Edward Albright. 'My character is a star varsity soccer player,' explained Taylor. 'And I'm gonna be able to use some of my martial arts.'

The series premiered on NBC on 13 October and Taylor appeared in seven of *My Own Worst Enemy*'s short run of nine episodes. The filming schedule combined with Taylor's *Twilight* commitments to ensure that his free time was more limited than ever, and meant that the young star was forced to sit exams out of high school, continuing his education through college classes.

The series proved short-lived, with no further episodes commissioned after the series finale aired on 15 December. While many critics praised the performances of a cast that included former *Twin Peaks* star Mädchen Amick and Mike O'Malley (best known for his extended run as Jimmy Hughes in the parenting comedy *Yes, Dear*), there was a widespread consensus that the series' plot was ambiguous to the point of opacity.

> **'We've met many different fans: the criers, who come around quite often; the hyperventilators who stop breathing and have to have a medic come. We've definitely seen some passion.'**
> **– Taylor Lautner**

Although *My Own Worst Enemy*'s cancellation was a disappointment, Taylor's focus moved quickly on. At the end of November he jetted off to Australia to fulfil further *Twilight* duties, and by the end of what had been a momentous year for the young star, his sights were firmly trained on reprising his role as Jacob Black in *Twilight*'s sequel, *New Moon*. Except this time, he'd be playing more than just a fleeting role in Bella's story. Hopeless, hollow and dead to the world, she returns to the reservation hoping to enlist Jacob's services as a mechanic, only to find a young man capable of fixing more things in her life than assorted parts of scrap metal. In stark contrast with the boy she remembers, Jacob Black is a changed man – in more ways than one. As Taylor himself revealed, 'I knew that Jacob's character transforms, not only emotionally and mentally, but also physically, so I immediately, the day after filming *Twilight*, hit the gym'.

Yet, daunting as they were, the physical demands of playing a hulking teen wolf in metamorphosis paled in comparison to the character's tangled relationship with Bella Swan. When she is abruptly abandoned by Edward, *New Moon* tells of the very darkest time in her life. As actress Kristen Stewart explained at Comic-Con 2009, what her character goes through is no ordinary break-up. 'Like, she literally is going to die . . . and the only thing that brings her out of it is this lightness [Jacob] brings.' Having shot to the heroic height of six-foot-five, the time is right for Jacob to step out of the shadows. 'He wants Edward out of the way so he can move in for the kill,' Taylor told *Interview* magazine's Michael Martin. The only question was whether Taylor himself would be ready to step up to the role of leading man, providing Robert Pattinson's lovelorn vamp with competition of the fiercest kind.

*Taylor takes a break from filming* New Moon *to attend Nickelodeon's Kids' Choice Awards in March 2009.*

# new moon
# rising
# 7

'I haven't noticed much of a change.
I grew out of a lot of my clothes, though.
I went from a men's small to a men's large.'
– Taylor Lautner

**T**wilight proved to be a runaway success at the box office. In its opening weekend the movie grossed a massive $69,637,740 in the US alone, rising to a global figure just short of the $400 million mark by the end of March 2009.

Critics often lean toward being less than enthusiastic about fantasy adventures aimed at teen audiences, but in *Twilight*'s case reviews were mostly positive. Writing for the *Guardian*, Peter Bradshaw declared the movie to be, 'Better and more convincingly acted than many of the ponderous grown-up "relationship" movies we have to sit through . . . It is, in its unworldly way, sweetly idealistic with a charm all of its own: a teen romance to get your teeth into.'

Legendary *Chicago Sun-Times* reviewer Roger Ebert was equally upbeat, noting: 'The movie is lush and beautiful, and the actors are well-chosen . . . *Twilight* will mesmerise its target audience.' In the *Los Angeles Times*, Kenneth Turan drew similar conclusions: 'This film succeeds, likely unreservedly for teens and in a classic guilty pleasure kind of way for adults, because it treats high school emotions with unwavering, uncompromising seriousness. Much as you may not want to, you have to acknowledge what's been accomplished here.'

Although Taylor's appearances as Jacob only occupied a small portion of the film's two-hour running time ('I'm only in three scenes in the first movie'), his performance was sufficiently memorable to draw praise. Reviewing *Twilight* for *Fangoria*, Jessica Leibe observed: 'Taylor Lautner does surprisingly well as Native American Jacob, though the sequels will provide him ampler opportunities to impress.'

As the early success of the film adaptation of the first of Stephenie Meyer's four-book series all but guaranteed that the subsequent instalments would be shot, the burning question for Taylor was: would he be re-cast as Jacob for *New Moon*? For his part, the young star was understandably keen. 'I'm trying not to think about it,' he told *About.com*'s

*A semi-clothed Taylor sets pulses racing in a scene from* New Moon.

Rebecca Murray. 'I mean Jacob's character becomes very cool and a lot more in-depth in the rest of the series. He's my favourite character. He's so cool.'

In *New Moon*, Jacob Black emerges from the background to become a key component of the continuing story, which represented a huge opportunity for Taylor to demonstrate a wider range of his talents than he'd been able to in *Twilight*. 'If there happen to be sequels, I really like Jacob's character when he's serious, because he gets so different. He almost has a split personality. When he is his normal self he's that happiest, friendly kind of guy, and then when he's a werewolf he's all intense and grumpy and Bella's just like, "Whoa! What happened to you?"' he told Mario Chavez in an interview for *Teen* magazine. 'So I look forward to that, as an actor, challenging myself to be able to show those two sides.'

> 'As soon as I finished filming *Twilight*, I knew I had to get to work right away; there could be no waiting involved. The day I finished *Twilight*, I came home and started bulking up.'
> – Taylor Lautner

However, until the filming of *New Moon* was officially confirmed, and its cast selected, Taylor had to endure something of an anxious wait. 'As much as you try not to, you always do, because you're like, "Oh my gosh, that would be so much fun and so cool,"' he admitted to MTV's Sabrina Rojas Weiss. 'But nothing's confirmed yet, so I try not to get my hopes up too high.'

Although he was by no means convinced that he would be cast, as soon as he had finished shooting the initial movie Taylor had taken an interest in how Stephenie Meyer's narrative developed. 'While I filmed *Twilight*, I wanted to focus on the book *Twilight* so I read *Twilight* before filming. Then when I got done filming *Twilight*, I started reading the second and third,' he told *canmag.com*'s Fred Topel. 'I mean, nothing's for sure yet, but we'll see. That'd definitely be cool.'

There was one major issue that served to throw Taylor's future as Jacob Black into doubt – his physique. At seventeen years of age Taylor had finished growing, but was yet to fill out. As *New Moon* charts Jacob's development from cute but clumsy Quileute-next-door to ferocious alpha-male, there was some concern that Taylor might be too slight to convincingly portray the strength and power of a ravenous lycanthrope. During one memorable moment in the book, Bella is struck by the sudden change in her childhood friend. 'Jacob had grown into some of his potential in the last eight months [. . .] His face was still sweet like I remembered it, though it had hardened too [. . .] all childish roundness gone.' And *New Moon* viewers needed to be similarly astounded by what they saw on screen, with the realisation of a rugged new Jacob to set hearts fluttering and temperatures rising.

On the plus side, Taylor could point to a proven track record of athletic excellence – as director Catherine Hardwicke discovered. 'They found a YouTube video of me on ESPN when I was eleven, and they were just freaking out and were watching it over and over again,' Taylor revealed. 'I said that it'd be cool if Jacob did some of that in the fight scenes. She said, "Yeah, that would be cool."'

*Above: Taylor comes face-to-face – and hand-to-hand – with his adoring public.*
*Below: Taylor, Kristen Stewart, and Robert Pattinson pose with their prizes at the 2009 MTV Movie Awards.*

*No pain, no gain: Taylor works out on the set of* New Moon.

With typical drive and application, Taylor refused to accept that a few positive words from *Twilight*'s director guaranteed his return as Jacob, and set about making sure that it would be difficult, if not impossible, to deny him the role on account of his physical stature. 'As soon as I finished filming *Twilight*, I knew I had to get to work right away; there could be no waiting involved,' he explained to *Interview* magazine's Michael Martin. 'The day I finished *Twilight*, I came home and started bulking up.'

In addition to adopting a high-protein diet, this process entailed Taylor spending many arduous hours at the gym. 'I knew where my character was going in the rest of the series, so obviously I knew I had some work ahead of me,' he told Talia Soghomonian of *Metronews.ca*. 'So as soon as I stopped filming *Twilight*, I got back home, hit the gym and worked very, very hard.'

As anyone who has attempted to 'bulk up' will attest, it's far from being just a question of piling on the protein and then sculpting muscle through intensive work-outs. If this were the case, competitive bodybuilding would not have had such problems with competitors choosing to cut corners through utilising steroids and other unwholesome methods of gaining muscle. Although Taylor had the benefit of a personal trainer – 'I did have a trainer that I used the whole time and I owe him a lot of thanks' – the process was not without its fraught moments. 'I was in the gym five days a week, two hours a day. At one point, I was going seven days straight,' he explained. 'I had put on a lot of weight, and then I started losing it drastically, so I was worried. It turned out I was overworking myself. My trainer told me that I couldn't break a sweat, because I was burning more calories than I was putting on.'

In many respects, Taylor's willingness to push himself to his physical limits – to the extent of endangering his health – was positive proof of his commitment to *The Twilight Saga*, demonstrating just how seriously he took his craft. In an age of prosthetics and computer-generated enhancements, few actors would be willing or able to summon the sheer strength of character necessary to endure such pain in order to meet the requirements of a particular role. Historically, those that do – like Robert De Niro, who gained an incredible sixty pounds for his portrayal of the ageing boxer Jake La Motta in the 1980 movie *Raging Bull* – tend to rise to the top of the profession.

In order to gain the weight and muscle tone necessary to convincingly bring the lupine Jacob to life, Taylor faced a constant struggle to maintain his regime. 'The hardest thing for me was the eating,' he recalled. 'At one point I had to shove as much food in my body as possible to pack on calories. My trainer wanted me to do six meals a day and not go two hours without eating. If I would cheat on eating one day, I could tell – I'd drop a few pounds.'

'Sometimes I look in the mirror and I don't recognise myself . . .
I don't even look like myself. But it's fun.'
– Taylor Lautner

After initially gaining a mere eight pounds in ten weeks, Taylor redoubled his efforts, with remarkable success. 'It's insane!' declared Ashley Greene, who plays Edward's adopted sister Alice. 'I was going through my phone and looking at all the pictures, and there's one from the wrap party that we did here after the first one and it's incredible. I was like, "Taylor, did you see this?" He was like, "Oh my gosh." He gained thirty pounds. He's not a little kid anymore.' Asked by *Interview* magazine's Michael Martin if his new physique was turning more heads, Taylor's answer was customarily self-effacing. 'I don't know. I should pay more attention to that. I hope so.'

Ultimately, all Taylor's hard work paid off and the news of his being re-cast as Jacob was announced via Stephenie Meyer's official website. This delighted the legions of fans who'd been campaigning for his return ever since they'd heard his tenure had been thrown into doubt. Indeed, rumours Taylor might be dropped in favour of some other 'random, less hot guy' had thousands of distressed Twilighters rushing to his virtual defence. Their comments – which can still be read on a dizzying array of online petitions – range from desperate pleas ('I'm gonna seriously freaking cry if they don't let him be Jacob'; 'I need Taylor Lautner!!!! Do you really want to kill me!!! He is a part of the movie and you can't take that away from me!!!'), to blatant threats ('If you don't keep him, I'll eat you!'), giving some impression of what it is to be intensely besotted by Jacob Black. Luckily, Summit Entertainment opted to give in to their demands, giving Twilighters more of what they were craving.

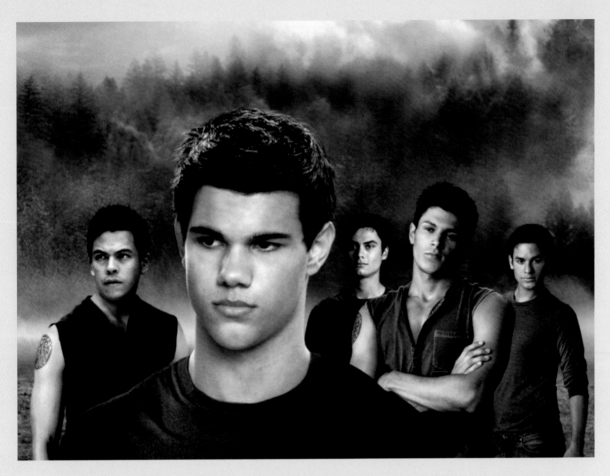

*Leader of the pack: Taylor (and from left), Chaske Spencer, Kiowa Gordon, Alex Meraz and Bronson Pelletier as members of the Quileute tribe with a dark secret in* New Moon.

However, such good news didn't mean that the newly buff star would be leaving the gym behind. 'Jacob's character is continually growing throughout the series,' he told *People*'s Scott Huver. He insisted that to match Jacob's development he would continue to improve his physique as the series progressed – whatever his own personal preferences.

> 'They're both talented directors, and I'm thankful that I had the opportunity to work with both of them.'
> – Taylor Lautner

'When we're done with the *Twilight* films I'll definitely bulk down and just get lean again because I don't want to stay big and bulky.'

Although he had succeeded in matching the physique necessary to portray the developing Jacob, there was little Taylor could do to bring himself up to almost seven feet tall – a reasonable height for a growing werewolf. But then few young actors could, and this was one instance where special effects would be required regardless of who was playing the role. When *buddytv.com*'s Kim Wetter interviewed the *New Moon* cast, she asked Taylor how he proposed to grow a couple of feet taller. 'I wish we had Catherine Hardwicke here to explain that one to you,' he replied. 'But we'll see. I'm doing the best I can.'

'He's going to stand on a lot of apple boxes,' joked Rachelle Lefevre. 'Peter Facinelli

*Taylor answers fans' questions and introduces exclusive footage from* New Moon *at 2009's Comic-Con International in San Diego.*

[who plays Edward's adoptive father, Dr Carlisle Cullen] said that I was going to use Tom Cruise's stilts,' Taylor added. 'We'll see what Catherine has under her sleeves. She's usually very creative.'

However, despite Taylor's expectations, Catherine Hardwicke was compelled to withdraw from directing *New Moon* due to scheduling conflicts with her forthcoming science-fiction thriller *Maximum Ride*, which is due for release in 2010. The in-demand director is also set to oversee a reworking of Shakespeare's *Hamlet*, based upon a screenplay by *Philadelphia* writer Ron Nyswaner.

On 13 December 2008, it was announced that Chris Weitz would direct what was now billed as *The Twilight Saga: New Moon*. Thirty-nine-year-old Weitz was best known for his work on such movies as *American Pie* and *The Golden Compass*, and was quick to make clear his respect for the *Twilight* universe. 'The extraordinary world that Stephenie has created has millions of fans, and it will be my duty to protect on their behalf the characters, themes and story they love,' he told MTV's Josh Horowitz. 'This is not a task to be taken lightly, and I will put every effort into realising a beautiful film to stand alongside a beautiful book.'

Although Taylor was sad to see Hardwicke depart, he quickly found that working with the dynamic New Yorker was great fun. 'Chris is amazing,' insisted Taylor. 'He's extremely talented and he's done a lot of amazing work. Everything is looking fantastic so far for this

the TWILIGHT saga
new moon

*A friend in need: The heartbroken Bella Swan (Kristen Stewart) is comforted by Jacob in a scene from* New Moon.

'It's completely understandable why they wanted to make sure he was right. He was so young, sixteen . . . I literally saw Jacob in him. I love that kid . . . I would do anything for him. I would kill for him, literally.' – Kristen Stewart.

and I know it's going to continue to. But at the same time, the set is so calm and relaxed and we're just having a really great time. Sometimes you wonder, "How is he doing this? How is he creating this beautiful work and we're just all having a blast doing it?" Chris has definitely taken control and he's a blast to be around.'

'They're both so talented in different ways,' observed Taylor when asked by *hitfix. com*'s Gregory Ellwood to compare the relative merits of Hardwicke and Weitz. 'What I love about Chris is the set is very calm and we're just having a lot of fun making the movie . . . At the same time, the conversations with Catherine – she just related to us so well. So does Chris. They're both talented directors, and I'm thankful that I had the opportunity to work with both of them.'

Taylor may have been delighted to be back on set as Jacob, but as the production got underway in Vancouver during March 2009, he immediately discovered one major downside to reprising the role – if Jacob was back, then so was his long black wig. 'The

*Nikki Reed, Taylor and Kristen Stewart take a stroll around Vancouver in March 2009, while on a break from filming* New Moon.

good news is when he transforms into a werewolf he cuts the long hair off, so I'd have regular hair,' explained a clearly relieved Taylor. 'Sometimes I look in the mirror and I don't recognise myself. It's an actual wig. It's glued to my head in the front and it gets itchy sometimes. You can see the lace if you look close, but it doesn't come across on camera. It gives me a totally different look. I don't even look like myself. But it's fun.'

'I'm excited to bring alive the new Jacob Black for the fans.'
– Taylor Lautner

In addition to a dramatic haircut and an even more spectacular transformation from boy to wolf, *New Moon* would see subtler changes for Jacob. 'He's a lot different than he was before,' confirmed Taylor. 'He transforms mid-story – in the first half, he's *Twilight* Jacob. I'm wearing a wig. My character's very clumsy, outgoing, and friendly. When he transforms into a werewolf, he becomes something very different. It's like I'm playing a split personality. Which is tricky, because sometimes I've had to play pre- and post-transformation Jacob on the same day of filming.

'I'm excited to bring alive the new Jacob Black for the fans. I'm really excited to be back with the whole team again and our new director, Chris Weitz. It's been a lot of fun so far and the movie's looking great, so I couldn't ask for more.

'I think the most important thing with Jacob is that pre-transformation, he's clumsy. He trips over his own feet. As soon as he transforms, he's very agile. At one point, he flings himself through Bella's window and lands at her feet, and that's the first time Bella realises this is a new Jacob. He never used to be this agile. I loved bringing out that side of him.'

Another key facet of *New Moon*'s plot is the burgeoning relationship between Jacob and Bella, deepening from friendship to something entirely more ambiguous. 'In *New Moon*, Edward leaves, and Bella needs someone to bring her out of this depression she's in, so she turns to her best friend, Jacob,' explained Taylor. 'It looks like it could go past friends. Bella's very confused. Jacob wants nothing more than to be more than friends. He wants Edward to get out of there so he can move in for the kill.'

The increasingly complex romantic triangle between Bella, Edward and Jacob enabled Taylor to stretch the emotional range of his acting. 'I also like a lot of the more serious scenes, the pivotal scenes in the movie, like Jacob and Bella's break-up scene, which is the first time Bella sees Jacob after he has transformed into a wolf,' he observed. 'And it's really emotional. I felt bad for Jacob just reading the books, but now that I'm actually living this character, I feel so bad for the guy! It's really sad.

'When I read the books, I felt bad for Jacob, because he can't have what he wants. I understand Jacob's pain.'
– Taylor Lautner

'Bella's torn. She's still in love with Edward, but she's kind of fallen for Jacob, too. When I read the books, I felt bad for Jacob, because he can't have what he wants. I understand Jacob's pain but also Bella's pain – how she's confused and torn between the two.

'Jacob's love for Bella is really intense. He will always be there for Bella, no matter what. Even if she's with another guy – or a vampire.' In particular, one scene between the two star-crossed lovers tickled Taylor's funny bone. 'The quote I love the most is Jacob's quote, "Does my half being naked bother you?"' he told MTV's Larry Carroll. 'That quote just cracks me up. Because you know, that's when he's shirtless, not wearing a top – we'll have to wait to see what he looks like.'

In contrast to the *Twilight*'s rain-swept Portland shoots, the *New Moon* locations in Canada and Italy were often bathed in sunshine – which is not always ideal when one is attempting to film a tale of vampires, werewolves and forbidden love. 'It's really funny because I think *The Twilight Saga* is the only movies where we have to stop filming when the sun comes out,' Taylor mused. 'So whenever it's sunny, we have to either go to an interior shot or just stop filming.'

Aside from being at the mercy of the climate, Taylor enjoyed making *New Moon* even more than he dug filming *Twilight*. 'It's fun playing characters not like yourself and being someone totally different for about three months,' he told Renata Joy of *Ultimatedisney. com*. In particular, the young star was delighted to be handed the opportunity to perform his own stunts. 'Basically you get an evaluation at the beginning of filming. They took me to a gymnasium to see what I could do. They put me on some dirt bikes to see how well I can do. I think they're just figuring out how much they're actually going to allow me to do. So far, I've been able to do everything, so I'm hoping that doesn't change too much, 'cause the stunts are a lot of fun.

'The bummer is, when he becomes a wolf, that's not actually me. When he does the cool fight scenes, he's transformed into CGI . . . I really enjoy the stunts so I had a lot of fun doing the dirt-bike sequences. I got to hop on the bike and go really fast and come to a skidding stop. It's really cool.'

One of the major advantages for an actor returning to film an ensemble-based sequel is that he or she will be acquainted with many of the other cast members, thus bypassing the sometimes tricky 'getting to know you' part of arriving on set. This was particularly true of *New Moon*, with Taylor, Kristen Stewart, Robert Pattinson, Ashley Greene, Edi Gathegi, and many others returning to reprise their *Twilight* roles. Such familiarity helped to foster a communal atmosphere, with many of the actors hanging out after a long day on the set. 'I have very early wake-up calls,' yawned Taylor. 'I'm usually waking up at 4:30 or 5:00, and we don't usually finish until about 5:00 or 6:00 at night. But we usually go out after, just explore the restaurants in town. It's been a lot of fun so far.'

> 'The coolest thing about the series is that we stay very true to the books; it would be silly for us not to, because the books are exactly what the fans want to see.'
> – Taylor Lautner

Like Catherine Hardwicke before him, director Chris Weitz was keenly aware of the passion that fans held for Stephenie Meyer's novels and ensured the movie stayed as close to the original text as the practicalities of filmmaking allowed. 'The coolest thing about the series is that we stay very true to the books; it would be silly for us not to, because the books are exactly what the fans want to see,' insisted Taylor. 'There's an action side to it, which I love, and there are werewolves now. There aren't just vampires. There's a wolf pack.'

The success of *Twilight* combined with the eternal popularity of Stephenie Meyer's four novels to ensure that fan interest in the making of *New Moon* was exponentially greater than what it had been for the first movie. 'It's the weirdest thing. Nobody really saw it coming,' marvelled Taylor. 'I mean, we knew we were making a movie of a very popular book, but we didn't know how well it was going to do. When it opened, it exploded, and that was not something any of us saw coming. Filming *New Moon* is a lot different than the first one because this time we know what we are getting into.'

Certainly, *Twilight* has shifted from being a notable publishing success story to becoming a global multi-media phenomenon, with magazines, newspapers and websites eagerly reporting the latest developments in the making of *New Moon* to the legions of fans in thrall to Meyer's stories of forbidden love. 'It puts a little more pressure on us than it did before,' admitted Taylor. 'But for the most part, it's been a blast.'

Having worked so hard to ensure that he could continue portraying Jacob, Taylor couldn't be happier with the direction his career has taken. 'I've been so busy with *The Twilight Saga* within the past year. It's been crazy, but it's been a lot of fun. We did tons of publicity. I got to travel to so many places in the world. I got to go to Australia, Tokyo . . . I got to go all over the place. So it's been a lot of fun. It's definitely keeping me busy though.'

*Taylor receives dirt-bike lessons in Vancouver*
*as part of his preparations for* New Moon.

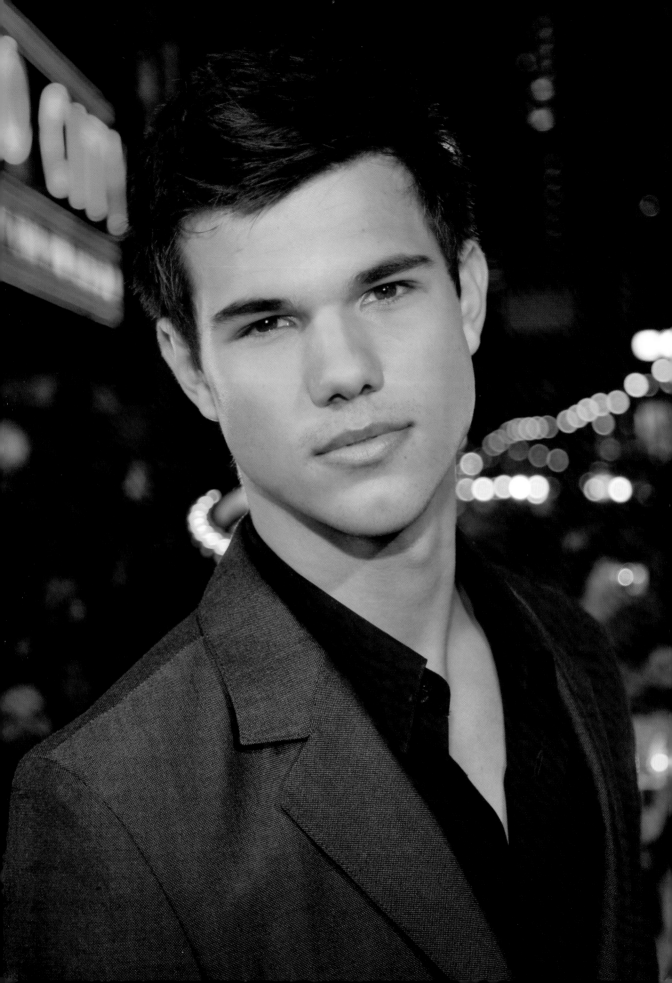

# star 8

'I've got a few years ahead of me.'
– Taylor Lautner

In July 2009, Taylor and his *Twilight* co-stars took time out to attend their second ever Comic-Con in San Diego. Back to face the same glaring lights, probing questions and worshipping *Twi*-fans as before, the cast must have been experiencing strong déjà vu as they took to the stage to present two tantalising unseen clips from *New Moon*. 'We know what we're getting ourselves into this time,' a denim-clad Taylor told *Fandango.com*, characteristically undaunted by the army of adoring Twi-hards who turned out for the screenings on the day. But, for all his understated charm, he'd forgotten one important detail.

The fans were still squealing in all the right places. 'Oh my God, this is gonna be awesome,' was just one of the delighted, ear-splitting cries as a certain young actor prepared to strip away his shirt. Except that this time, it was not Robert Pattinson's pallid physique on screen, but Taylor Lautner, speeding to Bella's rescue on a dirt bike, his mane of hair fanning behind him in the breeze. For Taylor as well as Edward Cullen's love rival, *New Moon* was the movie that changed everything. In November 2009 this second instalment of *The Twilight Saga* was unleashed on audiences everywhere, and Robert Pattinson's status as the series' only romantic hero staked and laid to rest.

With the premiere fast approaching, media interest in the film and its leading men reached uncharted levels of hysteria. For Taylor this represented something of a mixed blessing – on one hand his profile is now so high that his days of attending audition after audition in the hope of landing even the smallest TV role are history. Conversely, he's become a recognisable public figure, followed by hordes of infatuated Team Jacob members, whose every move is now being tracked by the paparazzi.

Although his parents have always sought to protect him from the downside of fame, there's little they can do to shield him from the extended reach of a telephoto lens. 'We're trying to teach him things, so that when he goes out on his own, he'll be prepared,' Dan

*Bright lights, big city: Taylor attends the 2009 MTV Video Music Awards in New York.*

*Taylor on stage at the 2009 Teen Choice Awards in Universal City, where* Twilight *dominated – winning eleven of the twelve trophies it was nominated for.*

Lautner told Terri Finch Hamilton of the *Grand Rapids Press*. But, even when he's home with his parents – an hour's drive out of Los Angeles – there's no escaping the ugly realities of life in spotlight for the sought-after teen star. Indeed, the worst of them are camped outside his door. 'There are twelve cars . . . outside my house,' revealed Taylor in an interview with *Teen Vogue*. 'You can't ever get used to it, because it's not normal to have people snapping pictures of everything you do. You just have to try not to let it affect you.'

Fortunately, the laid-back teen seems to be taking the intense scrutiny better than most. Much to Taylor's embarrassment, the work he's put in to maintain Jacob's swoon-inducing build has not gone unnoticed. In a matter of months – and a muscle-bound metamorphosis to rival anything experienced by Stephenie Meyer's wolf pack – the athletic young star has gone from scrawny to brawny. Showcasing the results in a variety of handsome *New Moon* promo shots, Summit Entertainment have ensured all eyes are on Taylor's enviable new physique, though the boy himself seems less than comfortable with this.

*Boxoffice* magazine wanted to know how the modest teen actor was coping with the sudden attention to his biceps. 'It's different,' he laughed, stressing that, rather than reasons of personal vanity, 'it was all for the job and that's all. I knew that Jacob was going

*Taylor and his one-time rumoured girlfriend, actress Selena Gomez,*
*go out for sushi in Vancouver during May 2009.*

*Ever the athlete, Taylor prepares to clear another of life's hurdles on the Los Angeles set of* Valentine's Day, *July 2009.*

to transform [. . .] and I wanted to portray him correctly for all the fans.' Despite this highly professional attitude to the role, though, Taylor admitted that he lives in dread of having one topic brought up over dinner with his parents – his steamy performance as a shirtless teen wolf. 'I'm hoping it doesn't happen because I'll start blushing.'

With his handsome features, rugged physique and deep-brown eyes, Taylor is fast becoming one of Hollywood's most eligible young bachelors, and any hint he's no longer single is seized upon by gossip-hungry editors. Fortunately, Taylor's level-headed approach to life and refreshingly humble opinion of himself has helped him deflect much of this prurient interest up to now. *Metronews.ca*'s Talia Soghomonian was the journalist to finally put the question burning in the minds of masses of *Twi*-fans. Jacob Black's only ever had eyes for Bella, but what does Taylor Lautner look for in a girl? His reply was typically down-to-earth. 'Somebody who can be themselves. Somebody who can just open up and be free and not try to be somebody different . . . I don't think I really know how to flirt,' admitted Taylor. 'I'm not out there or creepy like some guys are. I'll take my time and make sure everything is good, and that I really like the girl.' To the delight of Team Jacob members, he revealed that he'd be no more inclined to

'I don't think I really know how to flirt. I'm not out there or creepy like some guys are. I'll take my time and make sure everything is good, and that I really like the girl.'
– Taylor Lautner

*Left: Taylor in the audience of the Stanley Cup Final between the Detroit Red Wings and the Pittsburgh Penguins, June 2009. **Right:** Taylor Lautner, Kristen Stewart and Robert Pattinson introduce the third and final* New Moon *trailer at the MTV Video Music Awards in New York City, September 2009.*

date a famous actress than a fan-girl in the crowd. 'I don't exclude anyone . . .' he declared, making it known that his options are still very much open – in love as well as on screen.

However, despite Taylor's appreciation of the fact that, at seventeen years old, there is little need for him to rush headlong into a serious relationship, the media remain on constant watch for any sign that he may indeed have a girlfriend. In May 2009, *Film Fantasy* magazine ran a photo-feature under the headline '*Twilight Saga* romances blossom' that speculated as to whether or not Taylor had been secretly dating Selena Gomez, an adorable young actress-turned-singer, best known for her run as Alex Russo in the Disney TV series *Wizards Of Waverley Place*.

In addition to publishing photographs of Taylor and Selena out shopping in Vancouver (where both young stars were filming over summer 2009), and Selena enjoying some time with his younger sister Makena, the magazine gushed that 'their dating status seemed to be certified when Selena was photographed hanging out with Taylor's sister, Makena, and going to dinner with his parents. If a picture says a thousand words, then it sure looks like these young stars are on their way to a romantic relationship.' This was swiftly followed by *Life & Style* magazine running a picture of the couple in a brief clinch alongside quotes from a passerby who overheard Taylor telling Selena, 'You smell good.' A few weeks later, *OK!* magazine revealed to readers that Taylor had 'recently split with Selena Gomez'.

Such hyperbole represents a clear indication of the manner in which Taylor's rapid

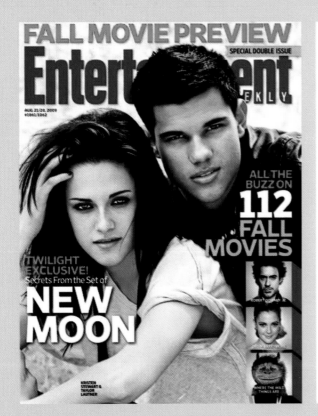

rise to stardom has placed him under a very public looking glass. One way the young star has found to escape the pressures of such scrutiny is to return home to Michigan. 'I love coming back here,' he declared. 'In LA, whatever you do for fun, you gotta spend money. Here, you go jet skiing on a lake. It's such a fun place for me. I go fishing with one set of grandparents, I go quad riding with the other set. We go trap shooting. It's so much fun . . . Here, people are way more down-to-earth.'

Despite his glittering achievements and the intense interest in his career and private life, Taylor remains a normal, unaffected teenager whose interests include sports, watching television and listening to music. 'Both of my favourite TV shows, *American Idol* and *The Contender*, just finished and I can't wait to see what's next for both of those,' he told *eFilmCritic.com*'s Jason Whyte. 'I don't really have that much time to listen to music, but I do like Outkast and Black Eyed Peas.'

With filming for *Eclipse*, the third instalment of *The Twilight Saga*, already underway – the cast regrouped in Vancouver in August 2009, exactly as planned – Taylor has geared himself up for many more arduous hours in the gym, reasoning that 'Jacob grows continually throughout the series so that means no matter if I'm doing a film or not, I'm going to have to put on a little bit more weight. I'll shoot for another ten [pounds]. We'll see what I can do, but I'll be working hard.'

As well as *Eclipse*, Taylor is also set to star in romantic comedy *Valentine's Day*, a film about the ways in which the pressures of the titular festival affect relationships. Directed by veteran filmmaker, actor and writer Garry Marshall, the movie also features *Pretty Woman* star Julia Roberts, Bradley Cooper (best remembered for his long run as Will Tippin in the TV series *Alias*), Jessica Alba (who played Sue Storm in the movie adaptations of Marvel Comics' *Fantastic Four*), and *Punk'd*'s Ashton Kutcher. *Valentine's Day* is scheduled for release in February 2010.

*'We knew what we were getting ourselves into this time,' Taylor knowingly said of his and his co-stars' decision to return for* New Moon.

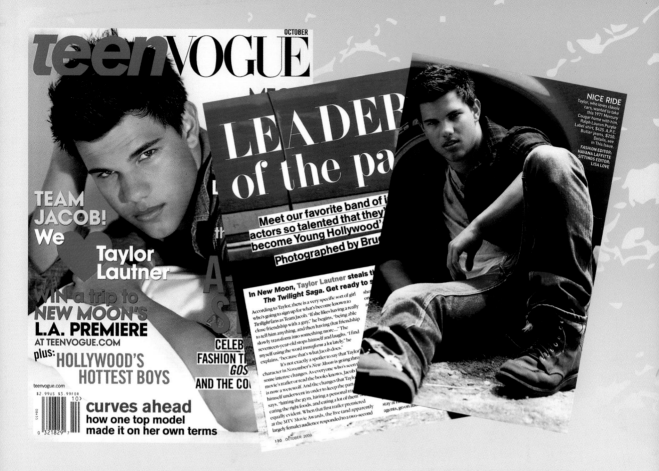

The movie represents the fulfilment of one of Taylor's longstanding ambitions – in November 2008 he was asked by *acedmagazine.com*'s John Delia which actors he'd like to work with. Predictably, starry-eyed Taylor chose his celebrity crush, along with a host of his own personal action heroes. 'I'd like to work with Jessica Alba, so I could meet her. I'd also like to do an action film maybe with Matt Damon or Mark Wahlberg. Those are some of the careers I look up to because I love action and drama.'

Taylor's youth means that, so far has his future career plans go, his options are almost limitless. Asked by *Interview* magazine's Michael Martin what he thought he would be doing if he hadn't become an actor, Taylor outlined the full scope of his possibilities. 'I always played sports when I was young. I played football and baseball for eight years. I loved football. So maybe I'd be doing some kind of sport. I also loved writing and directing. So maybe that could be in my future too. I'd love to get into that . . . Right now I'm an actor. But I could see that in my future.'

> 'I love coming back here. In LA, whatever you do for fun, you gotta spend money. Here, you go jet skiing on a lake. It's such a fun place for me . . . Here, people are way more down-to-earth.'
> – Taylor Lautner

'I'd love to do a movie with Denzel Washington, or some action star such as Matt Damon or Mark Wahlberg would be really cool, too,' he told *Vanity Fair*'s Adrienne Gaffney. 'Robert Rodriguez is great and I'd work with him again in a heartbeat.'

Yet, despite his taste for adrenaline-pumping action, Taylor has never been afraid to

*Taylor at the Teen Choice Awards, shortly before he and the rest of the* Eclipse *cast returned to Vancouver to begin shooting the third film in the series.*

*Director Chris Weitz advises Ashley Greene, Kristen Stewart and Taylor between takes on the* New Moon *set.*

'I loved writing and directing. I'd love to get into that . . .
Right now I'm an actor. But I could see that in my future.'
– Taylor Lautner

show his softer side, unashamedly naming *The Notebook* as one of his own favourite films. 'I don't think I should be embarrassed to admit it though – it's a great movie,' he said of this tale of lost love and tragic separation, concluding: 'I'm saying it proudly.'

Like the character that made him famous, Taylor is one young star who's always worn his heart on his sleeve. With all Hollywood pretense stripped away, there's nothing fake about the face he shows to the world. And perhaps it's this integrity – along with a deep empathy for Meyer's characters – that made him the perfect choice for Jacob Black. Displaying an emotional attachment to Stephenie Meyer's lovelorn teen wolf that's equally real, he spoke of his hopes for the release of *New Moon* and Jacob. 'I want [my fans] at the beginning of this film to see this really happy, nice, sweet guy that they fall in love with – and then all of a sudden – poof! – he's a completely different guy and not even the same dude.'

If the crazed hype surrounding the second instalment of *The Twilight Saga* is anything to go by, then he's already achieved the first part; stealing the hearts of a generation for Jacob and himself. The rest, however, is yet to be written.

But, however Taylor chooses to shape his own future, one thing's for certain: Lautner is a teen heartthrob with bite – and the drive and commitment to rise to the top. And, with sound advice from his parents, he's already learned all he'll need to make the most of the ride. 'We had no idea what was gonna happen,' Dan reflected on his son's part in the feverish *Twilight* phenomenon. 'We tell him, "You have no idea what's gonna happen tomorrow, so enjoy today. Have fun."'

*'We'll see what I can do,' Taylor said of his preparations
for the* Eclipse *shoot, 'but I'll be working hard.'*

British Library Cataloguing in Publication Data

Carpenter, Amy.
  The Taylor Lautner album.
  1. Lautner, Taylor, 1992 - Juvenile literature. 2. Motion
  picture actors and actresses - United States - Biography-
  Juvenile literature.
  I. Title
  791.4'3'028'092-dc22

  ISBN-13: 978-0-85965-453-1
  ISBN-10: 0-85965-453-2

Cover design by Coco Wake-Porter and Brian Flynn
Book design by Coco Wake-Porter with additional
artwork by Brian Flynn
Front cover photograph by Kevin Winter/Getty Images;
back cover photograph by Matt Baron/BEI/Rex Features
Printed by Scotprint

Acknowledgements
A book such as this cannot be completed without the help,
patience and perseverance of a lot of people. Special thanks
to our editorial team: Dick Porter, Laura Coulman and Tom
Branton. Thanks to our designers: Coco Wake-Porter and
Brian Flynn. Thanks to Harvey Weinig and Alice Morey for
researching material from the United States. The author
would like to thank Sandra Wake and Terry Porter.

    Taylor Lautner has given many interviews to newspapers,
magazines and websites, and these have proved invaluable
in chronicling his life and career. The author and editors
would like to give special thanks to *Grand Rapids Press,
Oregon Herald, Los Angeles Times, Seattle Post-Intelligencer,
The New York Times, The Times, Interview Magazine, Media
Blvd Magazine, Metro News, Teen Vogue, Teen Magazine,
Vanity Fair, The Guardian, E! Online, Sugar, Bliss, Love
Magazine, J-14 Magazine, Chicago Sun-Times, Fangoria,
People, Boxoffice Magazine, Life & Style, Film Fantasy,
OK!, Empire, Gone With The Twins, Entertainment Weekly,
GQ Magazine, Rolling Stone, Chicago Tribune, Eparsa
Magazine,* radiofree.com, efilmcritic.com, kidzworld.
com, karateangels.com, ultimatedisney.com, canmag.com,
taylorlautner.com, about.com, buddytv.com, reelzchannel.
com, acedmagazine.com, mtv.com, metronews.ca,
teamsugar.com, twilightmoms.com, hitfix.com, fandango.
com, movies.msn.com, ontheflix.com, newmoonmovie.
org, stepheniemeyer.com, twilightthemovie.com,
lionandlamblove.org, breaking-dawn.fr, eclipsemovie.
org, petitiononline.com, thepetitionsite.com, radaronline.
com, twilighters.org, thedeadbolt.com, taylorlautnerfan.
net, taylorfans.org, lautnerfan.net, lautnerfan.com,
taylorlautnersource.com, examiner.com, twilightcartel.
com, justjaredjr.buzznet.com. The following books were
used in research: *New Moon* by Stephenie Meyer, *Twilight*
by Stephenie Meyer, *Eclipse* by Stephenie Meyer, *Breaking
Dawn* by Stephenie Meyer, *Spirit Quest* by Susan Sharpe,
*The Robert Pattinson Album* by Paul Stenning.

    Thanks are also due to the film distributors: Summit
Entertainment, Dimension Films, Twentieth Century-Fox
Film Corporation, Karz Entertainment.

    We would like to thank the following for supplying
photographs: Corbis/Frank Trapper; Getty Images/
WireImage/ Kevin Mazur; Rex Features/BEI/Matt Baron; Rex
Features/c.Everett Collection; Getty/Stephen Lovekin; Rex
Features/Stewart Cook; Getty Images/FilmMagic/J. Merritt;
Getty Images/FilmMagic/Todd Williamson; Getty Images/
WireImage/SGranitz; Rex Features/BEI/Dan Steinberg;
Getty Images/WireImage/Barry King; Getty Images/Chad
Buchanan; Getty Images/WireImage/Todd Williamson; Rex
Features/Stewart Cook; Rex Features/Everett/c.Dimension;
Rex Features/Everett/c.Dimension; Getty Images/FilmMagic/
Chris Polk; Rex Features/Sipa Press; Getty Images/Kevin
Winter; Getty Images/Vince Bucci; Rex Features/BEI/Jim
Smeal; Rex Features/Everett/c.20thC.Fox; Getty Images/
WireImage/Casey Rodgers; Getty Images/WireImage/Charley
Gallay; Getty Images/WireImage/George Pimentel; Getty
Images/Frederick M.Brown; Getty Images/Charley Gallay;
Rex Features/Everett Collection; Bigpicturesphoto.com;
Getty Images/Kevin Winter; Getty Images/WireImage/Jordan
Strauss; Getty Images/Kevin Winter; Rex Features/Canadian
Press; Getty Images/FilmMagic/Chris Polk; Rex Features/
Masatoshi Okauchi; Rex Features/c.Everett Collection;
Getty Images/WireImage/Frazer Harrison; Rex Features/c.
Everett Collection; GettyImages/FilmMagic/Jeff Kravitz;
Getty Images/FilmMagic/Jon Kopaloff; Bigpicturesphoto.
com; Rex Features/c.Everett Collection; Getty Images/
FilmMagic/Michael Tran; Rex Features/c.Everett Collection;
Rex Features/c.Everett Collection; Bigpicturesphoto.com;
Bigpicturesphoto.com; Getty Images/WireImage/Kevin
Mazur; Bigpicturesphoto.com; Getty Images/WireImage/
Kevin Mazur; Rex Features/Johnny Lawrence; Getty Images/
Brad White; Getty Images/Christopher Polk; Getty Images/
WireImage/Jean Baptiste Lacroix; Getty Images/Frank
Micelotta; Rex Features/c.Everett Collection; Rex Features/c.
Everett Collection; *New Moon*/Summit Entertainment; *The
Adventures Of Sharkboy and Lavagirl*/Dimension Films;
*Cheaper By The Dozen 2*/Twentieth Century-Fox Film
Corporation; *Twilight*/Summit Entertainment; *Valentine's
Day*/Karz Entertainment.

    Every effort has been made to acknowledge and trace
copyright holders and to contact original sources, and
we apologise for any unintentional errors which will be
corrected in future editions of this book.